HOW TO STOP BEING TOXIC PLAYBOOK

TRANSFORM TOXIC BEHAVIORS, IMPROVE EMOTIONAL HEALTH, AND BUILD MEANINGFUL CONNECTIONS WITH 60 SIMPLE TECHNIQUES FOR PERSONAL GROWTH

WAYNE WATERS

© Copyright 2024 - Balance Press Publishing LLC

All rights reserved.

The content contained within this book may not be reproduced, duplicated or transmitted without direct written permission from the author or the publisher.

Under no circumstances will any blame or legal responsibility be held against the publisher, or author, for any damages, reparation, or monetary loss due to the information contained within this book. Either directly or indirectly. You are responsible for your own choices, actions, and results.

Legal Notice:

This book is copyright protected. This book is only for personal use. You cannot amend, distribute, sell, use, quote or paraphrase any part, or the content within this book, without the consent of the author or publisher.

Disclaimer Notice:

Please note the information contained within this document is for educational and entertainment purposes only. All effort has been executed to present accurate, up to date, and reliable, complete information. No warranties of any kind are declared or implied. Readers acknowledge that the author is not engaging in the rendering of legal, financial, medical or professional advice. The content within this book has been derived from various sources. Please consult a licensed professional before attempting any techniques outlined in this book.

By reading this document, the reader agrees that under no circumstances is the author responsible for any losses, direct or indirect, which are incurred as a result of the use of the information contained within this document, including, but not limited to, — errors, omissions, or inaccuracies.

CONTENTS

Introduction	iv
1. Self-Awareness and Reflection	1
2. Communication Skills in Person	16
3. Behavioral Changes	29
4. Relationship Building	40
5. Personal Growth	49
6. Emotional Regulation	58
7. Relationship Skills	69
8. Positive Reinforcement	79
9. Social Skills	88
10. Stress Management	96
11. Communication Skills in Texting	105
Free Bonus	116
Before We Wrap Up Your Transformation	117
Conclusion	119
References	123

INTRODUCTION

Change is hard at first, messy in the middle, and gorgeous at the end.

ROBIN SHARMA

Kevin always considered himself a good person. He had proven himself in his career and had earned an excellent reputation. But despite all this success, there was one area that he could not seem to get right: his relationships. Romantic relationships, friendships, and even professional connections appeared to follow the same frustrating pattern. They would start well, full of promise and excitement, but eventually, something would go wrong. Misunderstandings would escalate into arguments, trust would diminish, and before long, the relationship would crumble, leaving Kevin wondering what had gone wrong.

It was not until a close friend finally told him bluntly that he was the problem. "Kevin, you are toxic," she said exasperatingly. The words stung, but deep down, he knew she was right. He could see the patterns in his behavior—snapping at others when he felt stressed, holding grudges, refusing to apologize, and needing to be right at all costs.

Kevin realized he had been blaming everyone else for the problems in his relationships, never considering that his toxic behaviors might be the root cause.

This realization hit him hard. For the first time, Kevin understood that if he did not change, he would continue pushing away the people who mattered to him the most. He felt overwhelmed, unsure of where to start or how to break free from the destructive habits he had cultivated over the years.

Kevin's story is not unique. Many of us, at some point in our lives, have struggled with toxic behaviors, whether it is the inability to communicate effectively, a habit of holding onto resentment, or a tendency to lash out in anger. And like Kevin, many of us do not realize the damage we are causing until it is too late. The good news is you do not have to stay trapped in these patterns. You do not have to repeat the same mistakes, damaging your relationships and well-being. Change *is* possible, and it does not have to be complicated.

I have walked the path you are on. I remember the frustration and confusion of realizing my actions were causing harm. The *How to Stop Being Toxic Playbook* is your guide to transforming toxic behaviors and cultivating healthier, more meaningful relationships.

In this book, you will find 60 simple, practical techniques designed to help you quickly identify and change behaviors that are holding you back. Whether you struggle with anger, insecurity, toxic texting, jealousy, envy, or any other toxic habit, this playbook will give you the tools to make real, lasting change.

Each technique is designed to be straightforward and actionable, so you can start making improvements immediately—no more guesswork, no more wondering where to begin. This book aims to empower you to take control of your emotional health, improve your relationships, and build a life filled with positive, fulfilling connections.

My personal experiences and professional insights have led to the development of these effective techniques. I have faced the same struggles and found a way to change, and now I am here to help you do the same.

Embarking on a self-improvement journey can feel daunting, especially when dealing with the heavy burden of guilt and shame. These feelings can be paralyzing, making it difficult to see a clear path forward. If you have picked up this book, it is likely because you are tired of being labeled as toxic and are ready for a change. You are not alone. Many people face the same struggle.

When you are inundated with conflicting advice from countless sources, it is easy to feel overwhelmed. Which direction should you take? What methods actually work? This book cuts through the noise, providing simple yet powerful techniques to help you navigate toward healthier behaviors and relationships.

The reality is everyone makes mistakes. We all have moments where our actions or words cause unintended pain. What is important is recognizing these patterns and taking responsibility for your behavior. Change does not come overnight, but every small step counts. By acknowledging the issue and seeking resources like this book, you have already taken the first crucial step toward a better version of yourself.

My journey mirrors yours in many ways. I have experienced significant setbacks and the accompanying feelings of despair. Sometimes, I felt irredeemable, stuck in a cycle of negativity that seemed impossible to break. But through trial, error and persistence, I discovered strategies that genuinely work. These are not just theoretical concepts; they are tried-and-true methods grounded in personal experience and professional expertise. Trust me; if I can make these changes, so can you.

Keep Kevin's story in mind as you work through the techniques outlined in this book. Remember that change is possible, no matter how entrenched your habits may seem.

One of the most critical components of any transformational journey is understanding the importance of emotional health. Emotional well-being is not just about avoiding negative emotions but cultivating positive ones. It is about forgiving yourself and others, developing empathy, and building resilience. When you focus on improving your emotional health, you'll naturally find that your behaviors align with a more positive, conscious way of living.

Building and maintaining positive relationships is also crucial to personal growth and transformation. Sometimes, toxic behaviors can get in the way of our connections with others. Applying the techniques outlined in this book will help you nurture healthy and fulfilling relationships. Whether it is with your family, friends, or coworkers, you will see a significant improvement in the quality of your interactions. Not only will others see you in a new light, but you will also begin to see yourself more positively.

As you begin this journey, keep an open mind and be ready to embrace change. Some techniques may resonate with you more than others, which is perfectly okay. The goal is to keep moving forward, even if progress sometimes feels slow. Remember, real change is often incremental. Celebrate each small victory along the way and use it as motivation to keep going.

As you continue reading, get ready to engage in exercises that will help you reflect on your behaviors and identify areas for improvement. Don't worry; these exercises are not meant to make you feel bad about yourself; they are tools for growth and self-awareness. Use them as opportunities to learn and grow, understanding that every step you take brings you closer to the person you want to become.

Transformation can be challenging but immensely rewarding. The discomfort you may feel initially is a sign that you are stepping out of your comfort zone, which is necessary for your growth. Embrace the messiness of the middle phase, knowing that the result will be worth it. Your persistence will pay off in the form of improved emotional health, stronger relationships, and a more fulfilling life.

Are you excited to start this journey? Are you ready to let go of negative behaviors and embrace a fresh start filled with possibilities? If you are, let's take the next step together, flip the page, and dive in. We will work toward a healthier, happier you, one technique at a time.

CHAPTER 1
SELF-AWARENESS AND REFLECTION

Knowing yourself is the beginning of all wisdom.

ARISTOTLE

I was halfway through an intense text battle with my friend Jen when I had an epiphany. You know, the kind of fight where you furiously type out a three-paragraph response only to delete it because you know it will only make things worse? Yeah, that kind of fight.

It all started with a simple misunderstanding about dinner plans. I said I would be there at seven; she thought I meant six. Somehow, we were convinced the other was purposely trying to ruin the evening. As I reread my latest snarky text, something about how "real friends would not be so passive-aggressive," I had to pause. I mean, was I really this worked up over dinner plans?

But instead of hitting send, I did something radical: I put down my phone and took a deep breath. That is when it hit me—why was I so upset? Was this really about dinner, or was something else going on?

I started to notice a pattern. This was not the first time a minor miscommunication had escalated into a full-blown argument. In fact, I had a history of reacting like this. It was almost as if I was looking for reasons to get mad. That is when I realized I was not just upset about dinner; I was carrying around a lot of unaddressed stress and frustration, and it was seeping into my relationships.

So, I did something I had never done before: I called Jen instead of texting her. "Hey," I said, trying to sound more like a sane person and less like a drama king, "I'm sorry I overreacted. I think I have been carrying around a lot of stress and took it out on you."

There was a pause, and I braced myself for an equally heated response. But instead, Jen laughed—a real, genuine laugh. "I was thinking the same thing! I'm sorry, too. Let's just forget it and grab dinner."

It was like a weight lifted off my shoulders. Not only had I avoided a potential friendship-ending argument, but I had also gained insight into my behavior. I realized I had been allowing minor issues to turn into big problems because I was not dealing with my underlying emotions.

From that moment on, I made a pact with myself: No more toxic texting! If something bothered me, I would talk about it face-to-face or, at the very least, over the phone. I also started paying more attention to my feelings, asking myself why I was upset before lashing out.

It was not easy—old habits die hard, after all—but the more I practiced self-awareness, the less toxic my interactions became. I learned that sometimes, the best way to win an argument is not to have it at all.

Self-awareness is the cornerstone of personal growth and transformation. In your journey to overcome toxic behaviors and build healthier, more meaningful connections, the ability to reflect on your actions, thoughts, and emotions is paramount. Without self-awareness, you remain blind to the patterns that hold you back, the triggers that provoke your worst tendencies, and your impact on those around you.

So, if you find yourself typing a furious text or getting ready to snap at someone, take a step back. Ask yourself what is really bothering you. Chances are, it is not the person you are about to unload on. And trust me, recognizing that could save you a lot of unnecessary stress and maybe even a friendship or two. Self-awareness changes your relationships with others and your relationship with yourself. Once you start making those changes, you will wonder why you ever let your emotions get the best of you.

BUILDING SELF-AWARENESS THROUGH REFLECTION

Self-awareness and reflection are foundational to transforming toxic traits and behaviors. Without self-awareness, it is nearly impossible to recognize the negative patterns that may harm you and those around you. Reflection deepens this awareness, allowing you to examine your actions, thoughts, and feelings critically. Together, these practices create a feedback loop that leads to meaningful change.

Before we further explore the benefits of self-awareness and reflection in addressing toxic behavior, let's look at some typical toxic traits that people often exhibit. By recognizing and understanding these behaviors, you can begin to take proactive steps toward personal growth and improvement.

COMMON TOXIC TRAITS AND HOW THEY IMPACT RELATIONSHIPS

Toxic traits can manifest in many forms, often undermining relationships and affecting your overall well-being. Recognizing these characteristics is crucial for personal growth and can help you cultivate healthier connections. Below are some common toxic traits, including toxic texting habits, with explanations and examples to illustrate their impact:

MANIPULATION

This involves controlling or influencing someone's behavior or emotions to benefit yourself, often without the other person's consent. It can be subtle, such as guilt-tripping or gaslighting, making the other person question their reality. For example, saying to someone, "If you really loved me, you would do this for me," forcing someone to comply out of guilt or fear of losing the relationship. Constant manipulation can lead to feelings of inadequacy, anxiety, and low self-esteem. It diminishes trust and creates an unhealthy power dynamic, making relationships feel more like a battle than a partnership.

PASSIVE-AGGRESSIVENESS

This involves expressing negative feelings, resentment, or hostility in an indirect, non-confrontational way. Instead of addressing issues openly, a person might resort to sarcasm, procrastination, or subtle digs. For example, after an argument, they might say, "Oh, I guess you know everything now," instead of discussing their true feelings of hurt or frustration. This behavior creates confusion and tension, often leaving the other person feeling like they are walking on eggshells. It stifles open communication, leading to unresolved issues and festering resentment.

TOXIC TEXTING

This includes sending hurtful, manipulative messages to provoke a negative emotional response. This can also include constant criticism, ignoring texts (ghosting), using texts to control or monitor someone, or sending breakup texts. For example, sending multiple texts accusing someone of not caring because they did not respond immediately, using texting to bombard someone with negative comments, such as, "You are so selfish for not replying right away," or breaking things off via a text message. Sending a breakup text can be a form of avoidance, where the sender avoids a difficult conversation to protect themselves from uncomfortable emotions, leaving the recipient feeling blindsided and devalued.

In relationships, toxic texting can lead to heightened anxiety, stress, and a sense of feeling trapped. It diminishes the quality of communication, making it a source of dread rather than connection. Whether in romantic or professional relationships or friendships, toxic texting creates a barrier to open, honest communication. For example, in a romantic relationship, constant criticism or sarcasm over text can lead to feelings of resentment and insecurity, causing a rift between partners. In a professional setting, passive-aggressive messages can create a hostile work environment, damaging collaboration and morale.

BLAMING

This involves shifting responsibility for your actions or emotions onto others. Instead of owning up to your mistakes or addressing your feelings, you accuse others of being the cause of your problems. For example, say you forget an important event; instead of taking responsibility, you say, "You didn't remind me, so it's your fault I missed it," rather than accepting your oversight.

Chronic blaming damages relationships and promotes a cycle of defensiveness and resentment. Refusing to acknowledge your shortcomings and learn from them stunts personal growth.

JEALOUSY AND POSSESSIVENESS

Often driven by insecurity and the fear of losing control over someone, jealousy and possessiveness can lead to constant monitoring, questioning, or limiting the other person's freedom. For instance, constantly demanding to know where your partner is at all times or getting upset when your partner spends time with others, assuming it's a threat to your relationship. These behaviors create a suffocating environment where trust is absent, and the relationship is marked by fear and control rather than love and respect. It can lead to feelings of isolation and decreased self-esteem.

LACK OF EMPATHY

This is a common indicator of toxic behavior. A lack of empathy makes understanding and connecting with other people's emotions and experiences challenging. For example, imagine coming home upset after a difficult day at work. Instead of offering comfort or a listening ear, your partner responds indifferently, saying, "You are always complaining about work. It is not a big deal; just get over it." This dismissive attitude deepens the emotional rift between you and makes you feel unsupported and unloved, leading to long-term damage in the relationship. The same principle applies when showing a lack of empathy toward others, leaving them feeling unsupported.

SELF-AWARENESS: THE FIRST STEP TO CHANGE

Behavior change starts with identifying patterns and habits that no longer serve you. It requires self-awareness and a willingness to make conscious choices to shift your actions and reactions.

Self-awareness involves recognizing your thoughts, emotions, and behaviors in real time. It is about understanding why you react the way you do and how your actions impact others. When you know your triggers and patterns, you can begin to address the root causes of your harmful behaviors. For example, if you frequently get defensive and lash out when receiving constructive criticism, this defensiveness is often driven by a deep-seated fear of failure or rejection. Without self-awareness, it is challenging to realize this. You might simply believe that others unfairly attack you, which justifies your aggressive responses.

REFLECTION: UNDERSTANDING THE WHY

Reflection takes self-awareness a step further by encouraging you to think critically about your actions and their consequences. This process involves looking back at past situations to understand what triggered a toxic response, how it made others feel, and what you could have done differently. Reflection helps you identify patterns and consider alternative, healthier responses in future situations.

Self-awareness and reflection involve daily practices that help you understand yourself. These thoughtful activities uncover the layers of your thoughts, emotions, and behaviors, paving the way for significant personal growth. By engaging in regular self-assessment exercises, you can identify patterns and triggers that influence your actions, cultivating a deeper connection with yourself.

SELF-REFLECTION PRACTICE

Breaking the cycle of toxic behavior begins with acknowledging and understanding your toxic traits and how they affect you and others.

It is not always easy to admit our toxic traits, but taking responsibility for your actions is crucial for your growth and the health of your relationships. It is okay to feel overwhelmed or uncertain about where to start, but know that you are not alone in this journey. Committing to change means setting boundaries, building self-awareness, and finding healthier ways to handle difficult emotions and conflicts. It is a process that requires ongoing effort, self-reflection, and a willingness to learn and grow.

Let's explore some simple strategies that can help you cultivate self-awareness through daily reflection. By taking the time to pause and reflect on your thoughts, emotions, and actions, you can gain valuable insights into yourself and your life.

DAILY WRITING MEETS VIDEO JOURNALING

Journaling is one of the most powerful tools for processing emotions, gaining clarity, and tracking personal growth. It allows you to step back from your thoughts and feelings, creating a space to process them without judgment. By committing to daily reflection, you can better understand your toxic patterns, identify triggers, and develop positive thoughts and healthier behaviors.

Reflective writing serves as a mirror to your inner world. Each time you write, you uncover layers of emotions, past wounds, and unhealthy habits that might otherwise go unnoticed. Take a moment to think about what went well and what could have been better. Ask yourself questions like:

- Did I handle that situation the best way I could?
- Could I have responded differently?
- How did I feel at that moment? Was I happy, sad, or something in between?

By analyzing your interactions, you can identify your strengths and areas for improvement.

Celebrating your victories is important, for instance, when you stay calm during a disagreement or show empathy. This reinforces positive behavior. On the other hand, recognizing areas where you could have done better helps you to learn and grow. Writing about your interactions, feelings, and thoughts enables you to identify when toxic behaviors such as manipulation, defensiveness, or jealousy creep into your relationships. As you write, you gain clarity about the moments when you felt triggered, how you reacted, and whether your response was rooted in fear, insecurity, or unresolved trauma. Over time, you start to notice patterns, an essential step toward breaking the cycle of toxicity.

In addition to traditional journaling, video offers a unique, face-to-face interaction with yourself. When you speak openly to the camera, you can observe your body language, tone of voice, and emotional expressions. Watching yourself can be eye-opening; it allows you to see the moments when your toxic behaviors take shape, whether it is anger bubbling to the surface or a dismissive attitude in your tone. This visual form of journaling can deepen your awareness, making it easier to catch those behaviors in real time.

Reflective writing and video journaling create a balanced practice of self-awareness and growth. Writing gives you the space to explore your emotions and reactions with depth, while video journaling offers a visual reflection of how you present those emotions to the world. By combining these tools, you can consciously work on shifting toxic traits into healthier patterns, enhancing your relationships and emotional well-being.

To start, try dedicating 10-15 minutes each day to writing about moments when you felt emotionally triggered or acted in a way you later regretted. Once a week, record a short video journal where you talk about these experiences and reflect on how you can handle similar situations more mindfully in the future. With consistency, these practices will help you rewire your emotional responses and break free from the grip of toxic behaviors.

THE BENEFITS OF REFLECTION

Regularly reflecting on your thoughts and experiences can help you identify patterns and triggers in your behavior. By consistently writing down or recording your experiences and reviewing your reflections, you may notice patterns in how you react to certain situations. For example, you might realize that work deadlines or family gatherings always seem to trigger feelings of stress or anxiety. Once you recognize these patterns, you can proactively address or lessen these triggers. This could involve finding healthier ways to cope with stress, setting boundaries in certain situations, or seeking support from others.

Reflective writing goes beyond simply pointing out negative patterns; it also involves recognizing and appreciating positive ones. For example, you may realize that exercising or being creative positively affects your mood and productivity. This awareness allows you to incorporate more positive influences into your daily routine. By consciously identifying and adapting to positive and negative triggers, you gain a deeper insight into yourself, leading to personal growth.

Video journaling, on the other hand, offers a dynamic way to engage in self-reflection, allowing you to capture not only your words but also your facial expressions, body language, and emotions in real time. This will enable you to see the emotions behind your words. Speaking about your thoughts and feelings often brings out raw, unfiltered emotions, whether it is frustration, sadness, or joy. Seeing your true self can help you recognize when you are holding back or overly critical, offering a clearer picture of what's happening inside.

Sometimes, speaking out loud about difficult experiences can bring clarity. Video journaling allows you to voice thoughts and feelings that may be too difficult to write down. Talking through these emotions can give you insights into your mental and emotional state, and you can often find resolutions or understanding that might not emerge from writing alone.

PRACTICAL GUIDELINES FOR YOUR JOURNALING PRACTICE

To make the most out of reflection practice, here are some practical guidelines you can follow:

- **Dedicate time daily:** Set aside a specific time to write in your journal each day. Consistency is key to building a habit. You do not need to spend much time on it; just 10-

15 minutes can significantly impact your journaling practice.
- **Choose your medium:** When choosing between a traditional notebook and a digital app, consider which one you feel most at ease using consistently. The best option is the one that suits your preferences and habits. Take the time to explore both options and determine which one best aligns with your workflow and comfort level. Remember, the key is finding a tool you will be motivated to use regularly to maximize its effectiveness in helping you stay organized and productive.
- **Set clear goals:** Having a goal in mind for your journaling sessions can help give you a sense of purpose and focus. For example, explore specific emotions or experiences to understand them better. This can lead to a more insightful and meaningful journaling practice. Setting intentions for your writing can also help you track your progress and growth over time.
- **Be honest and authentic:** This is your personal space. Write honestly about your feelings and experiences without fear of judgment. Your words are safe here, and your feelings are valid. Let this be a place for you to be true to yourself.
- **Experiment with formats:** If your typical narrative writing gets boring, feel free to switch things up. Experiment with bullet points, incorporate Q&A styles or add drawings.
- **Regularly review your journal:** Periodically review your past entries. This will help you observe your progress, recognize patterns, and set new goals.

Remember that reflective writing goes beyond simply recording life events; it is about gaining insight and extracting lessons from those experiences. By engaging in reflective writing, you can develop a stronger relationship with yourself and enhance your self-awareness.

SELF-ASSESSMENT QUESTIONNAIRES

It is essential to recognize your challenges and areas for growth to cultivate self-awareness. Taking advantage of reputable questionnaires and quizzes can be a helpful method for pinpointing negative behaviors and habits. These resources use thorough research and psychological principles to guarantee accurate information about your personality traits and behaviors.

When choosing a questionnaire or quiz:

- Select ones that address your specific needs and can give you reliable feedback. There are many established resources created by psychology professionals that can be helpful. For instance, the Big Five Personality Test evaluates five key aspects of personality: openness, conscientiousness, extraversion, agreeableness, and neuroticism (Lim, 2023). This tool can provide insights into potential tendencies that may be linked to negative behaviors, helping you identify areas that need improvement.
- Once you have completed the quiz or questionnaire, reflect on the results. Take time to thoroughly analyze your findings and consider how they resonate with your experiences and behaviors. Seeking feedback from people you trust, like friends, family, or coworkers, can also be valuable. They may offer insights that confirm or question the results. Sometimes, the people in your life can notice trends in your behavior that you might overlook on your own.
- Once you have thoroughly reviewed the questionnaire results, creating an action plan to address any challenges you identified is essential. This plan should outline specific goals and steps to help you improve those areas. This could involve committing to better communication, considering therapy, or incorporating mindfulness practices into your routine. Ensure that your goals are SMART: specific, measurable, achievable, relevant, and time-bound. For

example, if you notice that negativity tends to impact your interactions, a SMART goal could be:
- "I will replace negative comments with positive or neutral ones during conversations" (specific).
- "I will track my progress by noting at least three positive or neutral comments I make daily in a journal" (measurable).
- "I will use mindfulness techniques to pause and think before responding to ensure my comments are constructive" (achievable).
- "Reducing negativity will help improve my relationships and create a more supportive environment" (relevant).
- "I will practice this daily for the next 30 days and review my progress at the end of each week" (time-bound).

By breaking down these goals into smaller, achievable steps and setting deadlines for yourself, you can stay focused and track your progress on your growth journey.

To enhance the reflection process, try using prompts that encourage a deeper exploration of your thoughts and emotions regarding your outcomes. Questions like "What caught me off guard in these results?" or "In what ways do these qualities manifest in my day-to-day activities?" can provoke profound self-reflection. As you go through this process of reflection, keeping a journal to write down your insights can also be advantageous. As mentioned earlier, journaling enables you to monitor your development over time and creates a space for ongoing self-analysis.

As you go through this process, remember that while reflecting on your own is essential, involving a coach or therapist can provide a valuable perspective. These professionals can help you make sense of your results and offer customized strategies for growth.

MINDFULNESS MEDITATION

Mindfulness practices can improve self-awareness and reduce stress. By focusing on present thoughts and emotions, you can gain valuable insights into your inner world, enhancing well-being and emotional balance.

To start practicing mindfulness, begin with short meditation sessions. Taking just a few minutes each day to sit in stillness can help establish a solid base for longer meditation sessions down the line. While it may be challenging to quiet the mind and stay focused at first, consistency is critical. Start by dedicating five minutes daily to meditation, focusing on your breath, and gently redirecting your thoughts back to it whenever they wander. According to research, even short periods of meditation can significantly reduce stress and improve overall emotional health (Kriakous et al., 2020).

If you are new to mindfulness, guided meditation is a great option. These sessions, usually facilitated by experienced practitioners or available through various apps and websites, provide structure and support to help you focus and stay engaged.

Incorporating mindfulness into your everyday life is vital to maintaining emotional stability and effectively managing your reactions to negative situations. Along with setting aside specific time for meditation, you can also practice mindfulness during routine activities like brushing your teeth, washing dishes, or taking a walk. By focusing entirely on these tasks and being aware of your sensations and surroundings, you can develop a more mindful way of being in all aspects of your life.

As part of your mindfulness practice, here is a short exercise that has helped cultivate awareness that will help you shift your focus when you feel overwhelmed or anxious.

Mindfulness Exercise

- Start by pinpointing what exactly is bothering you. Please give it a name so you can address it head-on.
- Make a list of things you can control and things you can't. This will give you clarity and help you focus on what you can change. Use the table below as a template to organize your thoughts. Take a step back, breathe, and enjoy the process.

What is in my control:	What is not in my control:
My mindset	My outcomes
My self-talk	Other people's actions
The boundaries I set	What happens around me
What I invest my energy in	Other's opinions
What I do when I encounter setbacks	Other's perception of me
What I invest my time in	The future
Being fully present in this moment	My past mistakes

KEY TAKEAWAYS

Self-awareness is the cornerstone of identifying and changing toxic behaviors. True transformation begins when you look inward, understand your actions, and acknowledge their impact on you and others.

Incorporating daily journaling and mindfulness practices into your routine is an effective way to cultivate self-awareness. Reflective writing or video journaling can help you capture your thoughts, feelings, and behaviors, helping you gain insight into yourself. This reflective process involves examining your life's positive and negative moments, which can help you recognize recurring patterns and triggers. Reflecting on your experiences and assessing your progress can give you valuable insights that will guide you toward self-improvement. Keeping a journal allows you to track your progress and identify areas where you can make necessary adjustments.

Additionally, incorporating mindfulness into your daily routine can positively impact your emotional well-being and stress levels. Start with short meditation sessions and gradually build up the time to establish a strong foundation for mindfulness practice. Being fully present and engaged in your activities helps to cultivate a mindful presence, leading to greater self-awareness.

Using the mindfulness exercise, you can recognize what is in your control and what is not, gaining greater awareness of what you should invest your time and energy in, improving your emotional health. This holistic approach offers a valuable tool for managing stress and promoting emotional balance.

Remember, self-awareness is not a solitary endeavor. Seeking support from trusted friends, mentors, or professionals offers valuable perspectives and guidance. Sometimes, we need an external viewpoint to see what we might miss on our own. Whether through therapy, coaching, or supportive relationships, these connections can help you stay accountable and offer encouragement as you work to transform toxic behaviors.

While self-discovery and growth can be challenging, they can be deeply rewarding, leading to improved emotional health, more meaningful connections, and a greater sense of well-being.

CHAPTER 2
COMMUNICATION SKILLS IN PERSON

Communication is the real work of leadership.

NITIN NOHRIA

In today's technology-driven world, there is no denying the importance of in-person communication. While our digital connections have their place, nothing can truly replace the authenticity and depth of face-to-face interactions. However, many of us struggle to make the most of these opportunities to connect on a deeper level.

In this chapter, we will talk about the art of effective in-person communication and how mastering this skill can significantly enhance your relationships. From learning active listening and responding thoughtfully to being present and engaged in your interactions, various strategies can help you make the most of your face-to-face interactions. By honing your ability to communicate effectively in person, you can cultivate more meaningful connections with the people around you. Whether it be a heartfelt conversation with a loved one or a business meeting with a colleague, your ability to communicate clearly and authentically can be the difference between building lasting bonds and resolving misunderstandings.

ACTIVE LISTENING PRACTICE

Have you ever been in a situation where you thought you heard someone say something, only to realize you misunderstood what they actually said? It happens to all of us at one point or another. It could be a misheard word, a garbled statement, or simply not paying close enough attention. Miscommunication is a common occurrence in daily life, but being aware of your listening skills and clarifying information can help prevent misunderstandings in the future.

Mastering the art of active listening is critical to improving your face-to-face communication skills. Active listening involves giving your full attention to the person you are talking to, reflecting on their words to show understanding, and refraining from interrupting or formulating a response while they are speaking.

To practice active listening:

- **Focus entirely on the person you're talking to without any distractions:** This means giving your full attention to them, setting aside any unrelated thoughts, and avoiding multitasking. When interacting with others, it's easy to get distracted by your phone, background noise, or even your thoughts. By eliminating these distractions, you show the person you're talking to that their message is important and worthy of attention. This focused attention is one of the foundational elements of active listening. By tuning in to what the other person is saying, you can better understand their message and offer a thoughtful response. This mindful approach promotes effective communication and deeper connections with others.
- **Reflect back on what you hear:** This involves repeating the message in your own words to show that you understand what is being said and to give the person a chance to clarify any misunderstanding. For example, if a colleague shares their concerns about a project deadline, you could say, "It sounds like you're concerned about meeting the deadline because of the workload." Reflecting helps

build better communication and understanding in a conversation.
- **Avoid interruptions or planning your response while listening:** Most people get distracted by thinking about what they will say next instead of actively listening to the person they are talking to. Interruptions not only disrupt the conversation flow but also convey a sense of disrespect to the person you're interacting with. Refraining from interjecting or preparing a response too quickly allows others to fully express themselves and contribute to a more respectful and collaborative communication environment. Remember, listening is just as important as speaking in effective communication.

THE BENEFITS OF ACTIVE LISTENING

Active listening involves more than just listening to what someone is saying. Nonverbal communication, such as maintaining eye contact, nodding in agreement, and using appropriate facial expressions, is equally important. These nonverbal cues show the person you are talking to that you are engaged in the conversation and value what they have to say.

Additionally, having an open body posture, like leaning forward or uncrossing your arms, can demonstrate your attentiveness and willingness to listen. These nonverbal cues help create a more meaningful and effective exchange of information.

Active listening has many benefits that can greatly improve communication in any relationship. Let's look at a few of these benefits:

- **It establishes trust between people:** When people feel truly heard and understood, they are more likely to trust you and feel comfortable sharing their thoughts and emotions. This sense of trust creates a foundation of security and mutual respect that strengthens personal and professional relationships.

- **It expands your viewpoint:** Remember that your perspective is just one of many. Opening yourself to other people's viewpoints gives you a broader understanding of life. Hearing different perspectives can challenge your beliefs and help you see things in a new light. It's a valuable way to grow and learn.
- **It enhances empathy and understanding:** When you truly listen to someone, you can gain valuable insights into their thoughts, emotions, and experiences. This level of empathetic understanding enables you to respond more effectively and compassionately, whether in a leadership role or just engaging in everyday conversations. For example, active listening equips you to address your coworkers' concerns and offer meaningful support in a work setting. In personal relationships, it allows you to cultivate empathy and be truly present in your interactions.
- **It reduces the chances of miscommunication:** Imagine a scenario where a couple, Jonathan and Sophia, are discussing weekend plans. Jonathan says, "I'd love to relax this weekend." Sophia interprets this as Jonathan wanting to stay home, so she cancels plans with friends. Later, Jonathan is disappointed and says, "I didn't want to cancel; I just wanted some downtime." If Sophia practiced active listening, she might have responded, "When you say you want to relax, do you mean you'd prefer to stay in, or do you still want to go out?" By seeking clarity and reflecting on what Jonathan truly meant, Sophia could have avoided the miscommunication, leading to a clearer understanding and a more satisfying weekend for them.
- **It helps ensure everyone is on the same page, reducing the likelihood of misunderstandings:** Misunderstandings are bound to occur when messages are not clearly conveyed or received. By reflecting on what you hear and seeking clarification, you can effectively minimize the risk of misinterpretation. This leads to more accurate

information exchange and prevents conflicts that may arise from communication breakdown.
- **It can help you cultivate patience over time:** It may take some practice and effort to become a good listener, but as you progress, you will find that your patience naturally grows as well. Allowing others to share their thoughts and feelings without interrupting or passing judgment cultivates a sense of understanding and empathy. Gradually, you will become more patient and compassionate toward others.

Practical Exercises

Here are a few valuable exercises to improve your active listening skills. These exercises will help you become more attentive and engaged in conversations.

Practice Role-Play With a Partner or in Groups

- Role-playing scenarios: Find an accountability partner or join a support group and take turns being the speaker and the listener. The speaker shares a story or problem, and the listener practices active listening by giving full attention, summarizing, and asking clarifying questions.
- Debriefing sessions: After each role-play, discuss what went well and areas of improvement. Focus on body language, tone, and how well you avoided interrupting or jumping to conclusions.

USE REAL-LIFE CONVERSATIONS FOR PRACTICE

Choose a daily conversation where you consciously practice active listening. Focus on maintaining eye contact, nodding, and giving non-verbal cues that show you're engaged. If you're unable to practice eye contact during role-playing with a partner, you can still do it on your own. A simple and effective exercise is to use eye contact drills by focusing on a person's eyes on a screen for four minutes. Here is how to do it:

- Find a video or image where the person is facing the camera directly.
- Sit in a comfortable position and focus solely on their eyes.
- Set a timer for four minutes and try to maintain steady eye contact throughout the session.
- Avoid distractions and stay present, noticing any discomfort or urges to look away, but gently refocus each time.

This drill helps you get accustomed to maintaining eye contact, building both your confidence and comfort in social interactions.

Also, practice mindful pauses in your role-playing sessions. During real conversations, practice pausing before responding to ensure you fully understand what was said. This helps reduce reactive or defensive responses that can lead to toxic communication.

SEEK FEEDBACK ON YOUR LISTENING SKILLS

- **Feedback circles:** After practicing active listening, ask your partner or group members for honest feedback on your listening skills. Ask them to highlight both your strengths and areas for improvement.
- **Self-reflection:** Keep a journal to reflect on your listening experiences. Note when you felt you listened well and when you could have improved and identify patterns in your behavior that may need change. You can integrate these exercises into daily interactions to gradually build better listening habits and reduce toxic communication patterns.

NONVIOLENT COMMUNICATION

What is your communication style? Are you manipulative, aggressive, or passive-aggressive? Have you thought about how your communication style impacts your interactions with others?

I once knew a guy named Larry who had a peculiar talent for turning every conversation into a competition. His friends called him "Larry the Last Word" because he always had to get the final jab in, no matter the topic.

One day, Larry and his friend Daniel were discussing something as harmless as the weather. Daniel mentioned that it looked like rain, but Larry, true to form, couldn't resist disagreeing. "Rain? Are you kidding? The sky's as clear as my windshield after I use Windex," he scoffed.

Daniel, who was used to Larry's antics, decided to play along. "Well, my knees are aching, and you know what that means—rain is coming!" he said with a grin.

Larry narrowed his eyes. "Your knees? Please, Daniel, that's just an old wives' tale. Next, you will tell me you can predict the stock market with a deck of cards!"

Daniel chuckled, but there was a slight edge to his voice. "You know, Larry, sometimes it is okay to just agree with someone."

But Larry couldn't help himself. "Agree? Why agree when I can be right?"

Daniel sighed and decided to change the subject to something more neutral—like their favorite pizza toppings. But even that did not go smoothly. Larry claimed pineapple was an abomination on pizza, while Daniel, a proud pineapple enthusiast, defended it with the zeal of a man protecting his firstborn child. What started as a friendly debate quickly turned into a heated argument, with Larry throwing out sarcastic comments left and right.

By the end of the day, Daniel was so fed up with Larry's constant need to win every conversation that he decided to take a break from their friendship. "I love you, Larry," Daniel said, "but talking to you is like playing dodgeball with insults, and I'm tired of getting hit."

Larry, stunned and alone, finally had the last word to himself. But as he sat there quietly, he realized that his habit of turning every chat into a verbal joust had cost him a good friend. Larry had nothing to say for the first time in a long time, and maybe that was exactly what he needed.

Communicating your needs, ideas, and opinions and resolving

conflicts peacefully are essential for building healthy relationships. Perhaps, like Larry, you tend to always think you're right; it is either your way or the highway. But I want you to remember that healthy relationships require compromise and open communication. It's okay to have differing opinions, but it is crucial to approach conflicts with an open mind, respect, and a willingness to find common ground. Building and sustaining healthy relationships takes effort and understanding.

Below are a few strategies for effective communication that have helped me improve my communication skills I genuinely believe will benefit you:

EXPRESS YOUR NEEDS WITHOUT BLAME

Communicating your needs without placing blame is a crucial skill for nurturing healthy and fulfilling relationships. When you express your desires or concerns without pointing fingers, you open up the opportunity for empathy, teamwork, and emotional security.

Blame often leads to defensiveness, hindering constructive dialogue and intensifying feelings of separation. On the other hand, taking ownership of your needs and sharing them clearly and respectfully promotes trust and mutual regard. This approach enables others to listen to you without becoming defensive.

One practical approach to achieve this is to use "I" statements, which focus on expressing your feelings and needs without placing blame on others. For example, instead of saying, "You never help around the house," you could say, "I feel overwhelmed when I have to handle all the chores alone." This shift in language can minimize defensive reactions and promote a more positive conversation.

"I" statements are effective because they keep the focus on your own emotions and experiences rather than directing accusations at the other person. This approach makes it easier for others to listen and increases their likelihood of understanding your perspective. Research shows that using "I" statements can lead to improved communication, stronger relationships, and more effective conflict resolution (Sehat, 2023).

VALIDATE OTHERS' PERSPECTIVE

Conflict resolution requires recognizing and validating the other person's perspective. When people feel heard and understood, they are more likely to engage positively in the conversation and work toward a mutually satisfying solution. Earlier, we discussed the importance of active listening and how it enhances empathy and understanding. To acknowledge someone's perspective, practice active listening by giving them your full attention, maintaining eye contact, and responding thoughtfully. For instance, if someone expresses frustration, you could say, "I understand that you're feeling frustrated because..." This shows empathy and allows you to validate the other person's feelings, making them feel heard and understood.

PRACTICE EMPATHETIC LISTENING

Practicing empathetic listening goes hand-in-hand with acknowledgment. Empathetic listening involves genuinely listening to understand the other person's feelings and viewpoints. One way to show that you are actively engaged in a conversation is through reflective responding. This involves paraphrasing or summarizing what the other person said to ensure you understand their message correctly. For instance, you might say, "It seems like you're feeling stressed about the upcoming project deadline. Is that right?" Such responses show that you are focused on the conversation and genuinely interested in their feelings.

APPLYING NONVIOLENT COMMUNICATION

The best way to develop and learn a new skill involves planning, practice, and self-reflection. Here are some effective steps to guide you through this process:

- **Identify and communicate your needs in a non-accusatory manner:** This allows you to resolve conflicts without hostility. Communicate your needs directly and avoid vague language. For example, instead of saying, "I need more support around the house," try being specific: "I need help cooking dinner two nights a week." This clarity helps the other person understand exactly what you need and how they can assist, reducing the potential for misunderstandings.

- **Frame your needs positively:** Instead of making demands, pose them as requests that allow room for discussion and flexibility. For instance, "Would you be willing to take on dinner duties on Tuesdays and Thursdays so we can share the workload better?" This approach encourages teamwork and demonstrates consideration for the other person's perspective and schedule.
- **Address common mistakes in communication:** One common mistake to avoid is using accusatory language, which can lead to defensiveness and exacerbate the situation. Instead, focus on expressing your emotions and needs without blaming others. Taking responsibility for your emotions can prevent misunderstandings and help others understand where you're coming from. Focusing on expressing your feelings and needs without placing blame on others can lead to a more productive and respectful conversation.
- **Be patient and avoid demanding instant solutions:** While it's natural to want to resolve conflicts immediately, it's crucial to recognize that some issues may take time to address. Give someone the space to process the conversation and return to it with a clearer mind if necessary. Following up on unresolved issues can also ensure you continue working toward a solution.

CONFLICT RESOLUTION EXERCISES

To master conflict resolution, it's essential to have strategies in place to address misunderstandings positively. When conflicts are handled effectively, they can lead to greater understanding and healthier relationships.

Below are some practical strategies you can use to address disputes constructively.

FIND COMMON GROUND AND USE PROBLEM-SOLVING TECHNIQUES

Resolving conflicts goes beyond trying to prove yourself right or making a point. It involves understanding other people's perspectives, communicating effectively, and finding common ground to reach a mutually beneficial solution. It's vital to approach conflicts with an open mind and a willingness to listen and collaborate rather than focusing solely on proving a point. When you shift your focus from winning the argument to understanding each other's viewpoints, you create a collaborative atmosphere.

Finding common ground, or areas of agreement, can provide a solid foundation for working through disagreements. Problem-solving techniques, such as brainstorming potential solutions or weighing pros and cons together, can promote a cooperative attitude. For example, say you have conflicting ideas on how to allocate resources for a project at work. Finding common ground by focusing on shared goals, such as meeting deadlines or increasing efficiency, can steer the discussion toward solutions that benefit everyone involved. These strategies encourage a collaborative environment where you consider and respect everyone's perspectives. This approach promotes a sense of understanding and appreciation for everyone's input.

MANAGE YOUR EMOTIONS

How often do you find yourself in a situation where a seemingly insignificant issue suddenly spirals into a heated disagreement? It's incredible how quickly things can escalate when emotions are involved.

Managing emotions effectively is critical to preventing escalation during disagreements. Emotional intelligence (EI)—the ability to recognize, understand, and manage your emotions, as well as empathize with others—is a vital skill that plays a significant role in our daily interactions. EI, which includes self-awareness and emotional regulation, is essential to resolving disagreements and misunderstandings.

EI enables you to identify and acknowledge your emotions but not let them dictate your actions. In challenging situations, having tools in place to manage your emotions effectively is essential. Techniques like deep breathing, taking a timeout, or reframing negative thoughts can be helpful in diffusing heated moments. For example, if you start feeling frustrated during a performance review or tense conversation, one powerful technique is the 4-7-8 breathing method. This involves inhaling through your nose for 4 seconds, holding your breath for 7 seconds, and then exhaling slowly for 8 seconds. Taking a moment to use this technique can quickly calm your mind, allowing you to gather your thoughts and respond thoughtfully rather than reacting impulsively (Gotter, 2018). You can download the 4-7-8 Relax Breathing app on the App Store and Google Play to guide you through this process. The app features simple designs and clear on-screen instructions, making it easy to follow.

SEEK FEEDBACK

Seeking feedback on your conflict resolution approach and continuously refining your techniques through workshops or training can significantly enhance your skills. Feedback provides valuable insights into how others perceive your conflict management style and effectiveness. Constructive criticism can help pinpoint areas for growth while also reinforcing positive behaviors. Workshops and training sessions centered on conflict resolution provide structured settings to hone these skills and opportunities for practice and peer collaboration.

Incorporating these strategies into your daily interactions will make dealing with conflicts more intuitive and less overwhelming. Consistently practicing these techniques can turn them into habitual responses, reducing the stress and anxiety that often come with confronting conflicts. For example, developing the habit of looking for common ground in everyday disagreement can help you cultivate a more cooperative approach to resolving disputes. Additionally, engaging in mindfulness exercises to manage your emotions can help you build resilience in confrontational situations. Over time, these practices will help you create a more harmonious and productive work or home environment.

KEY TAKEAWAYS

Mastering communication skills is one of the most powerful ways to enhance relationships and live a happier and fulfilling life. When you communicate with intention, clarity, and empathy, you create a space where trust can flourish, misunderstandings are minimized, and emotional bonds deepen.

The techniques I shared in this chapter, such as active listening, nonviolent communication, and conflict resolution, serve as bridges that connect you to others in more meaningful and authentic ways.

Active listening plays a significant role in improving face-to-face communication skills. Being fully present, mirroring what you hear, and refraining from interrupting is critical to effective communication. Utilizing non-verbal signals like maintaining eye contact and displaying an open body posture shows your interest and focus. The advantages of active listening go beyond simply understanding the other person's words; it helps establish trust, minimizes misunderstandings, and promotes better connections.

Effective communication allows you to express your needs and boundaries while also understanding other people's perspectives. This strengthens your relationships and reduces stress and conflict, leading to a more harmonious and balanced life. Whether in personal relationships, professional settings, or casual interactions, these skills improve how you relate to others and ultimately contribute to greater emotional well-being.

By consistently applying these techniques, you can nurture healthier relationships, increase your emotional intelligence, and create an environment where personal growth and mutual respect thrive. The more you practice, the more you realize that the foundation of any strong connection is communication that honors you and the people you care about. In turn, you enhance not only your relationships but also your quality of life.

CHAPTER 3
BEHAVIORAL CHANGES

Your behavior today is a reflection of your thoughts yesterday.

UNKNOWN

Change is always challenging, especially when it involves unlearning behaviors that have become ingrained over time. However, the fact that you're here, reading this, proves that you're ready for something different—a healthier way of living and interacting with others. Transforming toxic behaviors isn't about blaming yourself or getting caught up in shame; it's about recognizing the power you have to rewrite your story and create the meaningful connections you desire.

Behavioral change starts with awareness, followed by intention. Each small step toward healthier choices and more positive actions adds up, reshaping how you see yourself and the world around you. The path may be challenging, but commitment and the right tools lead to greater emotional well-being, stronger relationships, and a more fulfilling life. This journey isn't just about what you're walking away from—it's about what you're stepping into. Growth, freedom, and authentic connections are all worth looking forward to.

IDENTIFYING TRIGGERS

Recognizing and managing triggers is a crucial first step in breaking the cycle of toxic behaviors. Triggers, often rooted in past experiences or emotional wounds, can ignite automatic reactions that lead to harmful actions. By identifying these triggers, you can respond rather than react, creating space for positive change and healthier interactions.

To illustrate this, imagine Sarah, who has a fear of abandonment as a result of her childhood experience where her parents often left her feeling neglected. As an adult, Sarah notices that when her partner takes time to respond to her messages, she becomes anxious and angry. Without this realization, her emotional trigger (the fear of being abandoned) takes control, leading her to lash out at her partner with accusatory texts, even without a real threat.

By reflecting on this pattern, Sarah realizes how her fear drives her behavior. Understanding the source of her emotional trigger allows her to pause before reacting. Instead of sending a barrage of messages, she learns to manage her anxiety and communicates calmly with her partner.

Self-awareness is the foundation for healthier emotional responses and stronger relationships. It allows you to identify your triggers and empowers you to replace negative behaviors with mindful actions.

HOW TO IDENTIFY YOUR TRIGGERS

To overcome toxic behavior, identify what situations, people, or feelings cause you to react negatively. These triggers can often lead to behaviors like defensiveness, anger, or manipulation, which can create unhealthy patterns in your relationships. You can break away from these destructive cycles and form healthier connections by identifying them and learning how to manage these triggers.

Let's look at a few strategies you can use to identify your triggers and develop healthier emotional responses.

DOCUMENT SITUATIONS THAT TRIGGER NEGATIVE REACTIONS

The first step in identifying your triggers is documenting situations that trigger negative reactions. For example, you might notice that certain situations trigger a defensive or combative reaction. Situations like receiving critical feedback at work or feeling ignored by a loved one. Regularly documenting these moments can help you recognize the specific circumstances or emotions that tend to provoke negative behaviors. Keeping a journal or a digital note-taking app to record events that result in undesirable behaviors is an effective way to document these situations. Pay attention to details such as what happened, who was involved, and how you felt. By noting these factors clearly, you may start noticing patterns. For your reflective journaling practice, you can either go the traditional route or use a video journal to record your experiences, as discussed in Chapter 1.

ANALYZE PATTERNS AND COMMONALITIES

After gathering sufficient data, analyzing it can help you identify patterns and common factors that lead to certain behaviors. Look closely at your notes and see if any recurring themes or triggers stand out. Pay attention to specific people, locations, or times of day that are presented as provoking negative reactions. Are your reactions linked to feelings of rejection, insecurity, or fear? For example, the fear of abandonment could be a trigger that leads to toxic behaviors in your relationships. By recognizing these patterns, you start understanding the root of your reactions and finding effective ways to manage those triggers.

DEVELOP STRATEGIES TO MANAGE TRIGGERS

Now that you've identified your triggers, the next important step is to develop strategies to manage them effectively. One highly effective approach is through mindfulness practices. Research shows that mindfulness can help improve emotional awareness and regulation by encouraging non-judgmental present-moment awareness (Hofmann and Gómez, 2017). Engaging in activities such as sitting meditation, yoga, and mindfulness exercises can help you become less reactive and more reflective when faced with triggers.

The next time you encounter a trigger, try taking a moment to breathe deeply and refocus your attention on the present moment. This simple practice can help you maintain a sense of calmness and control and manage your triggers.

Another effective approach to managing your reactions to stressful situations is using cognitive-behavioral therapy (CBT) techniques, which are closely related to mindfulness practices. CBT techniques involve changing negative thought patterns, establishing healthy boundaries, and practicing self-compassion. For example, if a confrontation with a coworker often triggers feelings of anger, reframing your perspective and viewing it as a chance for both of you to learn and grow can lessen the emotional impact.

CREATE A PLAN TO MANAGE YOUR TRIGGERS

A written plan can be a practical guide to managing your triggers. This plan might include:

- identifying the trigger
- recognizing the emotion it provokes
- pausing to avoid an immediate reaction
- using a coping strategy, such as deep breathing, reframing the situation, or talking to someone you trust
- reflecting on the experience afterward to track your progress and make adjustments

Continuously working toward understanding and managing negative triggers requires dedication. Having a plan allows you to approach situations with greater calm and control, reducing the intensity of your toxic behaviors.

KEEP TRACK OF YOUR PROGRESS

Keeping track of your progress is essential for ensuring your strategies are effective. Keep a record of when you successfully manage triggers and think about how you can do even better. Keeping a log of each triggering event and how you dealt with it can help you see how you've improved over time. By focusing on techniques that work best for you, you can fine-tune your strategies for even better results. Reviewing your progress can also give you a motivating reminder of how much you've accomplished so far.

HABIT REPLACEMENT

Toxic habits, often born from pain, insecurity, or learned behavior, have a way of creeping into our lives and sabotaging our relationships, self-worth, and overall happiness. Whether lashing out in anger, manipulating others to feel in control, or engaging in negative self-talk, these habits can create a cycle of emotional damage that holds us back from truly connecting with ourselves and others.

But here's the empowering truth: Toxic behaviors aren't permanent. They're learned, which means they can be unlearned and replaced with healthier, more constructive patterns. Recognizing these habits for what they are—a defense mechanism that no longer serves you, opens the door to real transformation. Replacing toxic habits is about choosing to be better every day.

SUBSTITUTING TOXIC HABITS

When you're triggered, take a moment to think about your habits. For example, maybe you tend to get angry when you feel vulnerable or shut down emotionally when there's a conflict. Once you figure out what these habits are, try to think about what you could do differently. Instead of getting angry, try to communicate calmly. Instead of shutting down, express your feelings openly and honestly. By recognizing and changing these patterns, you can build healthier coping mechanisms.

Developing new habits requires practice. Start by setting small, attainable goals for yourself, like making healthier choices throughout your day. To help you stay on track, use reminders like sticky notes or alarms on your phone to keep these habits in mind. For instance, you could leave yourself a note on your desk to "take a breath before reacting" as a gentle reminder to pause and collect your thoughts before responding to stressful situations. Remember, consistency is vital when it comes to building new habits.

BUILDING POSITIVE HABITS

Developing positive habits is essential for personal growth. When you practice positive affirmations, you continuously remind yourself of the positive behaviors you are cultivating. For example, affirmations such as, "I can handle stressful situations calmly" or "I communicate in a kind and clear manner" can shift your mindset over time.

Additionally, tracking your progress, even the small wins, and celebrating each milestone can keep you motivated. Stay committed to your goals, and remember that every step forward brings you closer to your ultimate goal. Start by understanding the "why" behind building positive habits—knowing your purpose is vital. Once you have that clarity, establish a routine. To win the day, you must first win the morning, as everything begins with a solid, consistent routine.

MAINTAINING NEW HABITS

If you want to keep moving forward, ensure you have a good support system and someone to hold you accountable. Surround yourself with people who will encourage you no matter what and talk regularly with friends, mentors, or a therapist. Be bold and hold yourself accountable as well. Reflect on your habits occasionally and make necessary changes to ensure you're still heading in the right direction.

DAILY POSITIVE AFFIRMATIONS

How different would your life be if you changed your mindset? Imagine living a life filled with supportive, trusting, and loving family and friends. Picture the joy of setting and effectively communicating your boundaries. Envision the peace of mind that comes from surrounding yourself with positivity and mutual respect. Not only is it possible to live a fulfilling life, but it is also possible to build and nurture healthy relationships.

Positive affirmations are an effective tool for improving self-esteem and mindset. They can help you cultivate a positive self-image and reinforce your self-belief. By incorporating these affirmations into your daily routine, you can gradually shift your perspective, boost your confidence, and reduce negative self-talk.

When you practice positive affirmations, you continuously remind yourself of the positive behaviors you try to cultivate. For example, affirmations such as, "I can handle stressful situations calmly" or "I communicate in a kind and clear manner" can help shift your mindset over time.

Here are a few strategies to help you incorporate positive affirmations into your daily routine:

CREATE STATEMENTS THAT RESONATE WITH YOU

To begin with, create positive and empowering statements that are specific to your needs. Everyone's experiences and challenges are unique, so creating affirmations that resonate with you is crucial. For example, if you struggle with self-confidence, you could use affirmations like "I am confident and capable" or "I believe in my abilities." If you are impatient, your positive affirmation could look like, " I respond to challenges with patience" or "I am in control of my reactions. The key is to focus on areas where you need encouragement the most and create affirmations that are specific and meaningful to you.

PRACTICE CONSISTENTLY

Once you have your personalized affirmations, the next step is to incorporate them into your daily routine. One effective approach is to start the day with positive affirmations while looking in the mirror. For instance, saying, " Today is going to be a great day," sets the tone for the day ahead. Integrating affirmations into moments of quiet reflection, such as during morning coffee or before bedtime, helps solidify these positive beliefs over time.

Post affirmations on sticky notes around the house, set reminders on your phone, or even create affirmation cards to carry throughout the day. These can serve as a constant source of encouragement and positivity.

MOTIVATIONAL VIDEOS MEET AFFIRMATION AUDIOS

Developing a new habit requires constant practice. The best part about practicing affirmations is that you can use them in different aspects of everyday life. For example, during stressful situations, using statements like "I stay calm and focused under pressure" or "I trust myself to make the right decisions" can help you manage stress and maintain composure.

If you struggle with communication in your relationships, repeating positive statements like "I communicate with empathy and respect" or "I attract positive and uplifting people into my life," you can cultivate healthier and harmonious relationships.

The goal is to set intentions for the day. Take a moment to watch a motivational video or listen to an affirmation audio that speaks to your current needs. Don't hesitate to explore platforms online that offer these resources.

It doesn't need to be overwhelming - incorporating motivational videos and affirmation recordings into your routine, especially in the morning, can help kick-start your day. Keep it short and simple, and take time to reflect on the messages you've just absorbed.

Audio affirmations can help reshape how you view yourself, while motivational videos can spark determination and drive, encouraging you to stay focused.

Consistency is vital to make affirmations part of your daily routine. The more you practice positive affirmations, the more ingrained they become in your mindset.

Reflecting on the impact of your affirmations is equally essential. As you practice this new habit, take time to consider how your outlook and behavior have changed. Do you feel more confident? Is your self-talk becoming more positive? These reflections can motivate you to continue the practice and fine-tune your affirmations as needed.

THE BENEFITS OF POSITIVE AFFIRMATIONS

Practicing positive affirmations has numerous benefits. Studies show that regularly practicing affirmations can boost self-esteem, encourage positive thinking, and reduce negative self-talk (Moore, 2019). By frequently practicing affirmations, you gradually change your inner dialogue and cultivate a more optimistic outlook. This mental shift enhances your self-worth and improves your overall emotional well-being.

When you repeatedly affirm positive traits and capabilities, you internalize these beliefs, making them a natural part of your thought process. Research suggests that positive affirmations activate the brain's reward centers, specifically the ventromedial prefrontal cortex, which is associated with self-related processing and valuation (Hampton, 2019). This enhances your self-worth and resilience, making it easier to view otherwise threatening information more positively. Additionally, studies show that regularly practicing affirmations reduces stress levels and improves problem-solving abilities, further emphasizing their potential to improve mental and emotional health (Koosis, 2023.)

In addition to improving self-esteem and encouraging positive thinking, affirmations can significantly reduce negative self-talk. You can break the cycle of self-criticism and doubt by consciously replacing negative thoughts with positive affirmations. For instance, when faced with a challenging task, instead of thinking, "I can't do this," reframe that statement to, "I am capable of overcoming any challenge." Over time, this shift in internal dialogue promotes a more resilient and optimistic mindset.

Reflecting on your improvements and the challenges you face along the way is key to effectively practicing affirmations. Assess the changes you experience in your feelings, behaviors, and overall outlook since you made affirmations part of your daily routine. Acknowledging your progress and addressing any persistent challenges can help you fine-tune your affirmations to better suit your evolving needs. If certain strategies are no longer effective, adjust them to ensure they remain aligned with your goals.

KEY TAKEAWAYS

Transformation begins with self-awareness and a commitment to personal growth. As explored in this chapter, recognizing toxic patterns is critical to behavior change. The real transformation happens when you actively choose to replace harmful habits with healthier ones, focusing on growth rather than perfection.

Recognizing and understanding your triggers is vital to breaking the patterns that lead to unwanted behaviors. Keeping track of situations that trigger your reactions can help you identify the underlying causes, like certain people, places, or times that trigger your negative responses.

By practicing mindfulness, reframing negative thoughts into positive ones using CBT techniques, and setting goals, you can work toward making positive changes in your behavior and mindset.

The journey to change requires effort and dedication. Getting help from a professional gives you personalized advice and helps you fine-tune your approach. Sharing your experiences with people you trust can also help you feel supported and change your perspective on life.

Keeping track of your progress and thinking about how you've improved can keep you motivated, allowing you to make adjustments as needed.

Remember that change doesn't happen overnight. Toxic behaviors may have been ingrained over the years, influenced by past experiences, trauma, or emotional wounds. However, each small step you take toward change, whether it's setting goals for yourself, practicing positive affirmations, identifying your triggers, or managing your emotions effectively, can create a ripple effect that improves your well-being and relationships.

As you work through the techniques and insights we've discussed, be compassionate with yourself. Growth is never linear, and setbacks are natural. What matters most is your ability to acknowledge mistakes, learn from them, and continue moving forward with intention and self-awareness.

The more you invest in understanding yourself, the easier it becomes to break free from toxic patterns. This transforms how you relate to others and how you perceive yourself—building self-esteem, emotional health, and a more positive outlook on life.

By applying the lessons learned here, you set the foundation for a life filled with healthier relationships, greater inner peace, and a renewed sense of purpose. Every step you take is a testament to your strength and commitment to becoming the best version of yourself.

CHAPTER 4
RELATIONSHIP BUILDING

Relationships are the essence of life.

UNKNOWN

Relationships form the core of our existence. Whether with friends, family, or romantic partners, the quality of your connections deeply impacts your happiness, well-being, and sense of fulfillment. Building and nurturing solid relationships requires intentional effort, but the rewards—greater emotional connection, trust, and satisfaction are invaluable.

Meaningful relationships provide a safe space to share your feelings, challenges, and triumphs. People with strong relationships are better equipped to handle stress and can rely on their support network during difficult times.

Numerous studies show that having strong social connections lowers the risk of anxiety and depression (Seppala, 2014). Relationships offer emotional validation, a sense of security, and empathy, vital elements for improving mental health. According to research, people with strong social relationships have a 50% higher chance of longevity than those with weak connections (Harmon, 2010). In other words, being valued by others reinforces your sense of self-worth.

On the other hand, people without strong social support often struggle to manage stress effectively. Without trusted people to turn to, minor stressors can escalate into major sources of anxiety, resulting in social isolation and leading to feelings of inadequacy and low self-worth. Without consistent validation and support from others, you may begin to internalize negative thoughts about yourself, exacerbating issues of self-doubt and insecurity.

In this chapter, we will explore three crucial practices for building and strengthening relationships: spending quality time, giving genuine compliments, and performing acts of kindness. Relationships have a profound impact on mental, emotional, and physical health. Meaningful connections cultivate a sense of belonging, improve emotional resilience, and contribute to long-term health and happiness.

QUALITY TIME

At the heart of every strong relationship is quality time—moments spent with intention and focus. It's about being physically present and engaging in meaningful interactions. Whether through deep conversations, shared activities, or simply enjoying each other's company, quality time is a great way to bond with others.

In our fast-paced world, it's easy to get caught up in the hustle of everyday life; however, the essence of life lies in the quality of your interactions with loved ones. Engaging in activities that strengthen your connections does not mean only spending time together but also making it count. Whether participating in a shared hobby or collaborating on a project, these experiences create shared memories and deepen understanding. For example, cooking a meal together can turn a simple task into a chance to bond and work together. The act of preparing and enjoying food as a team gives you an opportunity to chat and work together, deepening your connection.

Additionally, one-on-one activities are crucial to maintaining solid relationships. Whether it's scheduling date nights or having family game nights, the key is to spend quality time together without any distractions. Setting aside specific times for these moments creates lasting memories and strengthens your emotional bonds. Studies show that couples who prioritize these kinds of activities tend to have higher levels of relationship satisfaction and intimacy (Hogan et al., 2021).

Here are a few strategies for making the most of your time with your loved ones:

FOCUS ON MEANINGFUL CONNECTIONS

Meaningful interactions go beyond hanging out with someone; it's about understanding and caring for each other. Engaging in open and honest conversations allows the people in your life, whether it's your partner, friends, or family members, to freely express their thoughts and feelings, creating a safe space for vulnerability. Active listening plays a crucial role in these dialogues. When you genuinely listen to someone without jumping in with your thoughts right away, it shows that you respect their feelings and experiences.

ENGAGE IN SHARED ACTIVITIES

Outdoor activities are a great way to escape from the fast-paced world and spend quality time together. Whether it's hiking, picnicking, or biking, these activities are an excellent opportunity to disconnect from the digital world and reconnect with each other. Such experiences can also reduce stress and improve your mental well-being while strengthening your bond. Regularly engaging in these kinds of activities can improve your relationships, allowing you to enjoy all the benefits that come with it.

PRIORITIZE QUALITY OVER QUANTITY

Focusing on quality time spent together rather than just the quantity is essential to maintaining relationships. It's not just about the amount of time you spend together but how you make the most of that time. Meaningful and focused interactions can significantly impact more than simply being in the same space for hours. This concept applies to all types of relationships, whether it's with your partner, family, or friends. Ensuring that the time you spend together is engaging and meaningful can strengthen the value of your relationships.

Let's look at a few ways to enhance your interactions:

SCHEDULE ACTIVITIES AHEAD OF TIME

To prioritize quality time, schedule your activities ahead of time. In today's busy world, it is easy for relationships to take a backseat to other responsibilities. By intentionally carving out time in your schedule for loved ones, it becomes easier to maintain consistent, meaningful interactions. This may mean setting aside specific times of the day or week exclusively for spending with family, friends, or your partner.

EMBRACE THE POWER OF BOUNDARIES

Setting boundaries is another important aspect of maintaining the quality of interactions. Creating device-free zones or times can help minimize distractions and build genuine connections. For instance, having a no-phone rule during dinner can encourage everyone to engage in conversation and share about their day. These simple yet effective practices can enhance the depth and authenticity of your time together.

Technology-free evenings are particularly beneficial for romantic relationships. When you put away your screens, you can give each other your full attention and really connect on a deeper level. Whether you're reading together, playing board games, or having a good conversation, these activities can bring you closer as a couple and strengthen your bond even further.

ENGAGE IN NURTURING CONVERSATIONS

Supportive conversations are another key element of spending quality time in relationships. Being there for each other during difficult times, offering a listening ear, and providing emotional support can significantly strengthen your relationships. Through these moments of vulnerability and trust, relationships thrive.

Balancing your time between work, family, and self-care can be challenging. However, nurturing your relationships requires spending quality time with the people you care about and taking care of yourself. This might mean turning down other obligations to ensure you have enough time for your loved ones.

Spending quality time together can create beautiful memories. Whether you're going on a last-minute trip, celebrating important milestones like birthdays and anniversaries, or enjoying fun activities together, these moments become treasured memories that bring you closer. Celebrating successes and special occasions as a team adds depth to your relationships and helps everyone feel loved and supported.

The impact of spending quality time on mental health and well-being cannot be overstated. Meaningful relationships provide comfort and offer support during difficult times. Having supportive people you can rely on creates a foundation for emotional stability that enhances your overall well-being.

COMPLIMENTING OTHERS

Think back to when you received a genuine compliment from someone —perhaps it was about your hard work, your kindness, or even a talent you often overlook. How did that moment make you feel? The warmth of their words likely washed over you, filling you with a sense of pride, validation, and appreciation. Any self-doubt or insecurities you may have carried faded for a brief moment, and you felt genuinely seen and valued. That simple act of recognition might have shifted your entire mood, inspiring you to continue on your path or even motivating you to reach higher.

Genuinely complimenting people is essential to forming deeper connections and encouraging positive interactions. Complimenting someone isn't just about saying nice things for the sake of it. When you give specific and sincere compliments, you recognize someone's efforts and unique qualities. This kind of praise is much more meaningful than just empty flattery. By giving genuine compliments, you show others you value and appreciate them. For instance, instead of just saying, "You're great," try being more specific and saying something like, "I really admire your perseverance." This shows you have taken the time to appreciate and recognize something special about that person.

THE BENEFITS OF GENUINELY COMPLIMENTING OTHERS

Compliments can uplift spirits, create deeper connections, and remind us that what we do and who we are matters. When people receive validation for their actions or attributes, it:

- **Enhances their self-worth:** This can lead to deeper connections with friends, family, or coworkers. For example, telling a colleague, "You handled that difficult client situation really well," can uplift their mood and motivate them to keep up the good work.
- **Encourages positive interactions and behavior:** When you acknowledge and appreciate someone's hard work, they are more likely to keep it up and interact positively with others. It's like a domino effect of good vibes that helps everyone involved. Just telling someone they bring positive energy to meetings subtly encourages them to maintain that uplifting demeanor in future interactions.
- **Improves self-concept:** Complimenting someone is a great way to make them feel good about themselves. Compliments help build understanding and create stronger connections between people. For instance, in a work setting, telling a coworker how much you appreciate their effort on a project can improve your working relationship and encourage teamwork. These little gestures add up over time, fostering a positive and respectful environment.

Reflecting on the impact of your praise helps reinforce its authenticity. Before giving a compliment, please take a moment to consider its potential effect. Is it coming from a place of genuine appreciation, or are you simply trying to fill silence with pleasantries? Authenticity is key in ensuring that your praise is received as intended. For instance, telling someone, "Your advice helped me through a difficult time," after honestly reflecting on how their words made a difference in your life, conveys genuine gratitude.

Avoiding flattery is essential in maintaining the integrity of your compliments. Flattery often comes across as insincere and can undermine trust. Giving genuine compliments is better based on what you observe and feel. For example, if a friend has been there for you when you went through a difficult time, it's more meaningful to say something like, "I really appreciate how you've been by my side no matter what," instead of just saying, "You're amazing." Showing genuine gratitude and acknowledging specific acts of support goes a long way in building trust and stronger relationships.

And remember that positive reinforcement doesn't just benefit the other person; it enriches you also.

ACTS OF KINDNESS

Acts of kindness have a profound impact on the relationships we build throughout our lives. Small, thoughtful gestures performed regularly can promote a positive environment. Whether it's holding the door open for someone, smiling at a stranger, or listening attentively to a friend in need, these acts cultivate a culture of generosity and reciprocity. They show others that you care about their well-being and contribute to an atmosphere where everyone feels valued.

These small gestures may seem insignificant, but their collective power is far-reaching. By extending kindness to others, we create a cycle of goodwill that can permeate our communities.

HOW TO PERFORM ACTS OF KINDNESS

Kindness demonstrates care and consideration for others and often sparks a ripple effect, encouraging others to reciprocate and spread kindness. Below are a few ideas on how to perform acts of kindness:

- **Help others without expecting anything in return:**
Offering to help purely out of the goodwill in your heart

enhances social connections and reinforces bonds built on trust and mutual respect. Small gestures like helping a neighbor with groceries, offering a ride to a colleague, or simply lending an attentive ear can significantly impact your social interactions. These selfless acts benefit the person receiving help and bring a sense of satisfaction and happiness to the giver—you. Expectations can sometimes cloud our intentions in relationships. By helping others without any strings attached, you eliminate transactional dynamics and focus on genuine care and support. This approach demonstrates that your actions stem from a place of sincerity and empathy, building more profound, more authentic connections. Over time, this practice encourages a supportive network where people feel comfortable relying on you.

- **Express gratitude and appreciation:** Taking the time to acknowledge and thank those around you for their contributions strengthens your bonds and promotes a positive atmosphere. Writing a heartfelt note, giving a sincere compliment, or verbally expressing thanks to the people who support you can go a long way in showing your appreciation. These expressions of gratitude make others feel valued and recognized, leading to more harmonious and satisfying relationships. Gratitude is a powerful tool in nurturing relationships. It shifts your focus from what you lack to what you have, promoting a sense of contentment and positivity. Expressing gratitude regularly promotes happiness by cultivating a mindset of abundance and appreciation.
- **Volunteer or support community initiatives:** Engaging in activities like serving meals at a homeless shelter, participating in environmental clean-up efforts, or mentoring disadvantaged youth allows you to connect with others who share similar values and goals. These shared experiences help strengthen communal ties and make you feel part of something larger than yourself. Community

involvement provides opportunities to meet new people and build relationships based on shared interests and values. It also offers a chance to give back and make a tangible difference in the lives of others.

Incorporating small, thoughtful gestures into your daily routine can promote a positive environment and strengthen relationships. A simple smile, genuine compliment, or helping someone brings joy and fosters a sense of connection. Making a habit of showing kindness regularly becomes a natural part of how you interact with others. This can create a ripple effect of positivity and goodwill that spreads to those around you.

KEY TAKEAWAYS

Relationships are the foundation of a fulfilling life, and building strong connections requires ongoing effort, intentionality, and care. By spending quality time, giving genuine compliments, and practicing acts of kindness, you can create more meaningful bonds with the people around you.

Spending quality time with your loved ones creates special memories and strengthens your connection. Whether you're doing something fun together or simply focusing on each other, these moments make life richer and bring you closer.

When you prioritize meaningful interactions over just being around each other, you build trust, empathy, and a real sense of closeness. Setting aside regular, distraction-free time to spend with your loved ones increases your satisfaction with your relationships and helps them flourish even more.

These practices enhance trust, emotional connection, and mutual respect, ensuring your relationships continue to grow and thrive. Ultimately, the essence of life lies in the relationships we cultivate, and through mindful actions, you can nurture and strengthen them for years to come.

CHAPTER 5
PERSONAL GROWTH

Personal growth is the key to unlocking your full potential.

UNKNOWN

Imagine sitting in a room where you don't have to pretend, where there's no judgment, and you can share your most painful thoughts and not hide them. Therapy creates such a space—a safe environment to dig deep and confront the roots of toxic behaviors that affect your relationships and self-worth.

Toxic patterns often stem from past wounds, unresolved trauma, or emotional defenses that developed over time. In therapy, those layers begin to peel away. The behaviors you've been stuck in start to make sense, and with the help of a professional, you finally understand the "why" behind your actions. However, therapy doesn't stop at understanding—it's a transformative journey toward personal growth, where you develop new tools to break toxic cycles and rebuild healthier relationships with yourself and others.

Therapy is not a quick fix; it's a commitment to doing the hard, necessary work for growth. It offers an empowering opportunity to rewrite your story, guiding you out of destructive habits and into a life marked by emotional clarity, compassion, and meaningful connections.

As you begin this chapter, ask yourself: *What could change in my life if I allowed myself to heal?*

THE ROLE OF THERAPY OR COUNSELING

Working with professionals to address personal problems is critical to growth and unlocking your full potential. Therapy is one of the most effective ways to help you break free from toxic behaviors and achieve long-term emotional health. Working with a professional provides structure, accountability, and a safe environment to explore deeper emotional patterns and behaviors.

If your behaviors are a result of underlying emotional wounds, such as past trauma, seeking therapy is a vital step. A therapist can help uncover the root causes of toxic tendencies, which often lie buried beneath the surface. Whether it's a licensed counselor, psychotherapist, or clinical social worker, a professional can offer both support and practical guidance as you work toward personal transformation.

For example, if you struggle with anxiety or depression, therapy can help you identify your triggers and develop coping mechanisms to manage these conditions more effectively (Rosenblatt, 2021).

Here are a few guidelines you can follow if you choose to work with a professional:

FIND A QUALIFIED COUNSELOR OR THERAPIST

Finding a counselor or therapist who is a good fit for you is crucial. Different types of therapists specialize in various areas, like cognitive behavioral therapy, psychodynamic therapy, or humanistic approaches. Researching and choosing a therapist who is an expert in your issues will ensure you get the best treatment possible. For example, if you're dealing with trauma, you may benefit from seeing a therapist who specializes in trauma-informed care.

Finding a therapist whose communication and personality style resonates with you is also important. When you're comfortable with your therapist, you develop a trusting relationship, which is vital for successful therapy.

DEVELOP STRATEGIES TO MANAGE TOXIC BEHAVIORS

Once you have found a suitable therapist, the next step is to use therapy sessions to develop strategies for managing toxic behaviors. In therapy, you can work on identifying your toxic behavior patterns and understanding their origins. Your therapist can guide you in developing healthier ways to interact with others and manage conflicts. For instance, if you usually get defensive during disagreements, therapy can help you learn to communicate openly and constructively.

SET CLEAR GOALS

It's essential to have clear goals in mind when starting therapy and be actively involved in the process to make real progress. What do you hope to achieve? Do you need a boost of confidence to manage stress or improve your communication skills? By sharing these goals with your therapist, they can customize your sessions to fit your personal needs. And remember, being open and honest about your experiences and feelings during therapy will help you get the most out of it. For instance, if you want to improve your self-esteem, your therapist might assign activities like journaling positive affirmations or practicing challenging negative thoughts when they pop up. Doing these exercises outside of your therapy sessions can solidify your progress and make it easier to incorporate those new, positive habits into your everyday routine.

BE CONSISTENT

Additionally, attending therapy regularly and consistently keeps the momentum going. It takes time and sustained effort to achieve lasting change, and attending therapy sessions infrequently can hinder your progress. Consistently showing up for your sessions and putting in the effort shows your dedication to the process and gives you continuous support and guidance from your therapist.

Remember that therapy is not a quick fix. It's more like a journey of self-discovery and personal growth. Be patient with yourself in the process. Sometimes, change happens slowly, and you may need to confront difficult emotions and memories along the way. But in the end, the benefits are significant. Therapy can lead to profound transformation, helping you develop resilience, self-awareness, and emotional stability.

Seeking professional help to address underlying issues and gain insights is a powerful step toward personal growth. Finding a qualified counselor or therapist who meets your needs ensures you receive the appropriate support and guidance. By setting clear goals and actively participating in your therapy sessions, you can make the most out of the experience and improve your overall well-being.

RESOURCES FOR PERSONAL GROWTH

Self-help books are a valuable resource for personal growth. While therapy provides personalized guidance, self-help books offer additional knowledge and practical advice you can apply at your own pace. Reading self-help books is a great way to keep learning and growing. It's a highly effective strategy to reach your full potential. Reading the right books teaches you much about emotional intelligence, self-improvement, building meaningful relationships, and changing negative behaviors.

The first step in this journey is to select books on emotional intelligence (EI) and personal development. EI—the ability to understand and manage your emotions and recognize and empathize with other people's emotions—can help you develop better social skills and improve your overall emotional health. There are plenty of self-help books, like this one, that can help you on your personal growth journey.

When picking out books to read, choose reputable authors. Take someone like Brené Brown, for example. She's known for her work on vulnerability and empathy and earned a reputation as a trusted voice in the world of personal growth. Her book, *The Power of Vulnerability*, discusses how authenticity can help us connect with others and improve our emotional skills (Brown, 2012). Daniel Goleman's work can also give you insight into how to improve your emotional intelligence. By reading his books or articles, you can gain valuable insights that make a big difference in understanding and managing your emotions. These authors share valuable insights that can help you develop your emotional regulation skills and better relate to others.

After choosing the perfect books, it's vital to implement the advice offered in your everyday life. Take, for example, Daniel Goleman's findings on emotional intelligence. He stresses the significance of self-awareness, self-management, social awareness, and relationship management *(Daniel Goleman's Emotional Intelligence Theory*, 2013). For example, you can practice self-awareness by regularly reflecting on your emotions and identifying your behavior patterns through journaling. You can apply self-management by setting goals for emotional regulation, for instance, practicing deep breathing when you feel overwhelmed. You can develop your social awareness by practicing active listening and showing empathy when interacting with others.

To apply the knowledge, you learn from self-help books and build self-awareness:

- **Pay attention to your feelings and recognize any recurring behaviors:** Journaling or practicing mindfulness meditation are effective ways to achieve this. You can benefit from the wisdom found in these books by putting these practices into action.
- **Reflect on the insights you gained from reading:** After reading a book, take some time to reflect on how you can apply the knowledge and techniques you've learned to your life. For instance, if a book discusses the importance of empathy in building strong relationships, consider your recent interactions where you could have shown more empathy. What could you have done differently? Think about how this change could have made a difference in the outcome. By engaging in regular reflection, you can

reinforce new habits and behaviors, making them an integral part of your daily routine.
- **Share the insights you've gained with others:** It reinforces your understanding and can also help those around you grow and develop. Discussing what you've learned with friends, family members, or colleagues can spark meaningful conversations and create opportunities for mutual support. For instance, you might share a particularly impactful concept from a book with a friend who is struggling with similar issues. Sharing ideas can lead to deeper connections and collective growth.

WORKSHOPS AND SEMINARS

Attending workshops and seminars is a powerful way to enhance your skills and motivation. By engaging with new ideas and experiences, you unlock your full potential.

Let's look at some of the benefits of attending events that focus on improving communication and personal growth:

- Workshops and seminars often cover various topics, such as effective communication, emotional intelligence, leadership, and self-awareness. By participating in these events, you can learn valuable skills that benefit you in various aspects of your life. For example, a communication workshop might give you advice on how to become a better listener or improve your conflict resolution skills. Additionally, workshops on personal growth often have activities that can enhance your self-awareness and confidence. These events give you a safe place to learn about your strengths and weaknesses, helping you understand yourself and how you interact with others.
- They are an opportunity to meet like-minded people. Attending workshops and seminars allows you to meet people who share your interests and can significantly expand your support system. Meeting people who share similar

goals and interests can be incredibly motivating. It's an opportunity to network with people who understand your journey and can offer support and encouragement. Studies show that people actively engaging in professional development are more likely to stay excited and driven to achieve their goals (Parsons, 2022). Professional development opportunities, such as workshops and seminars, expose you to new ideas and expertise, cultivating an environment of continuous learning and growth. Networking offers ongoing support, mentorship, and even collaboration opportunities, leading to lasting relationships. For instance, you might start a conversation with someone who becomes your mentor, offering valuable guidance and advice to help you on your personal growth journey.

- Actively participating in these events is key to getting the most out of them. This could involve taking notes, asking questions, and getting involved in discussions and activities. Applying the knowledge you gain to all areas of your life is crucial to your growth. For example, let's say you attend a workshop on emotional intelligence. If you only listen without getting involved, you may not get as much out of it as you would if you actively participate and apply what you learn to your everyday life. But if you actively participate and practice the techniques taught, such as recognizing and managing your emotions, you're more likely to see positive results.

CHOOSING THE RIGHT EVENTS

Another important step in your personal development journey is researching and selecting workshops that align with your goals and interests. Not all workshops will benefit you, so choosing those that will be valuable to you is vital. For instance, look for workshops focusing on communication skills to improve your communication. On the other hand, if you're looking to improve your leadership abilities, search for workshops that will help you develop those skills. Attending different workshops is a great way to gain new perspectives and insights. It can broaden your horizons and teach you a lot. For example, if you attend workshops on how to be a better leader in a hybrid work environment, you can learn about the latest trends in your field and sharpen your skills.

Choosing the proper workshops and events to attend ensures that you invest your time and resources wisely. So many options are available, from in-person seminars to online webinars, so it's crucial to pick ones that will genuinely help you improve. Conferences and workshops bring together different professionals, allowing you to learn new skills and expand your network. By carefully selecting the events you participate in, you can make the most of your experience and continue to grow—personally and professionally.

KEY TAKEAWAYS

Overcoming toxic habits requires more than just a desire to change—it demands a conscious, sustained effort to rewire deeply ingrained behaviors. Therapy, self-help books, and workshops are three powerful avenues that provide the guidance, tools, and community support you need to make lasting changes in your life.

Therapy provides a safe space to explore the root causes of your struggles, offering valuable insights into your behavior and thought processes. By gaining a deeper understanding of the root causes of your toxic habits, you can develop personalized strategies to confront and manage them. Therapy also provides accountability, ensuring that your progress is permanent and transformative. Working with therapists and counselors sets you on a journey of self-discovery and can improve your interactions. Setting clear goals and actively engaging in therapy is crucial to your progress.

Additionally, utilizing self-help books and attending workshops and seminars is essential on your transformative journey. Self-help books provide practical advice on emotional intelligence and personal development, while workshops offer hands-on experiences to help you build essential skills. Networking with like-minded people during these events expands your support system and encourages continuous learning.

By actively participating in therapy, reading self-help books, and attending workshops, you are investing in your emotional health and equipping yourself with the tools to break free from toxic patterns. Each of these resources complements the other, creating a holistic approach to transformation. The journey to overcoming toxic habits is not easy, but with the proper support and dedication, you can reclaim your emotional well-being and build a healthier, more fulfilling life.

CHAPTER 6
EMOTIONAL REGULATION

Emotional regulation is the ability to manage your emotional state and actions.

UNKNOWN

Mike considered himself the picture of composure—except when it came to one thing: traffic. He could handle a hard day at work, losing a game of golf, and even his buddies roasting him, but get him on the freeway during rush hour, and it was a different story. One afternoon, after a long week, Mike found himself stuck behind a driver going 10 miles under the speed limit. As his grip tightened on the steering wheel, he felt his blood pressure rise.

"Come on, buddy! Are we driving to the grocery store or the moon?" he yelled, fully aware that the other driver couldn't hear him.

But then, just as he was about to hit the horn like it owed him money, he remembered something his wife had told him about emotional regulation. She joked, "Mike, it's either your blood pressure or learning to chill. Your choice." He smirked, took a deep breath, and cranked up his favorite rock song instead of laying on the horn.

As the music blared, he imagined himself in a cheesy action movie where he was the hero saving traffic from the slow driver. He chuckled to himself, picturing the absurdity. By the time he reached his exit, the anger had faded, replaced by a weird sense of victory. He didn't lose it. He regulated his emotions.

Later, when Mike told his buddies the story, one of them joked, "So, Mike, does this mean you're finally Zen now?"

Mike grinned. "Nah, just smarter. My blood pressure's got plans for the weekend."

Think for a second: How often do you find yourself getting upset or frustrated in certain situations? Perhaps, like Mike, getting stuck in traffic on your way to work irks you, causing you to arrive at the office already in a bad mood. Learning to control your emotions can help you handle situations better. Emotional regulation is key to a healthier and happier life.

EMOTIONAL REGULATION TECHNIQUES

Relaxation techniques are an effective way to deal with life's ups and downs. From anxiety to anger, methods like deep breathing, muscle relaxation, and mindfulness can calm the body's physical response to stress, giving your mind the breathing room needed to regulate your emotions.

Below are a couple of relaxation techniques you can use to regulate your emotions during stressful times.

DEEP BREATHING EXERCISES

Deep breathing is one of the simplest yet effective emotional regulation techniques you can incorporate into your daily routine. It's particularly useful if you need help with conflicting advice or are struggling with recurring negative behavior patterns. Deep breathing exercises help calm your mind and relax your body, bringing you into the present moment.

Let's look at some breathing techniques you can practice during stressful times:

DIAPHRAGMATIC BREATHING

Practicing diaphragmatic breathing is an effective technique for controlling your breath. Most people take shallow breaths that only reach the chest, but deep breathing engages the diaphragm—the muscle beneath your lungs. This relaxation technique maximizes oxygen intake and expels carbon dioxide more efficiently, which has physical and emotional benefits (Cunningham, 2018).

To practice diaphragmatic breathing:

- Lie down on a flat surface with your knees bent and your head supported.
- Place one hand on your upper chest and the other below your rib cage.
- Inhale slowly through your nose, allowing your stomach to rise while keeping your chest relatively still.
- Exhale slowly through pursed lips, engaging your stomach muscles to help control the exhalation. Try to keep your chest as still as possible while you breathe out.

As you get used to this technique, you can practice it while sitting or standing. The key is to breathe deeply into your abdomen using your diaphragm rather than your chest. It can be challenging at first, but practicing consistently will make this form of breathing more natural over time.

GUIDED BREATHING EXERCISES

Structured guided breathing exercises can help you learn proper breathing techniques. These exercises often include audio or visual aids to help you maintain focus and ensure you are performing each step correctly. Guided breathing exercises can be greatly beneficial if you're new to deep breathing practices, as they provide instruction and motivation.

As discussed in Chapter 2, breathing exercises such as the 4-7-8 technique can help you destress and relax. To practice the 4-7-8 technique, inhale through your nose for a count of four, hold your breath for seven counts, and then exhale through your mouth for eight counts. This technique helps you regulate your breath and calms the nervous system, making it an effective tool for stress management.

Another relaxation exercise you can use is box breathing. This technique involves inhaling for four counts, holding your breath for four, exhaling for four, and holding again for four. Repeat this cycle several times to experience its calming effects.

INTEGRATING DEEP BREATHING INTO MINDFULNESS PRACTICE

Incorporating regular deep breathing exercises into your daily mindfulness practice can significantly enhance your emotional health. Mindfulness practices encourage paying attention to the present moment without judgment, and focusing on your breath is a simple yet powerful way to anchor yourself in the now.

Consider setting aside a specific time each day for deep breathing. You can integrate it into your morning routine to start your day with calmness and clarity or to unwind and relax before bedtime. Consistency is the key to experiencing the benefits of relaxation exercises.

You can use guided meditation apps that feature breathing exercises or set reminders throughout the day to pause and take a few deep breaths to guide you throughout the process. Over time, these moments of focused breathing will become a natural part of your day, improving your overall well-being.

EMPLOYING DEEP BREATHING IN STRESSFUL SITUATIONS

In moments of heightened stress, the body's natural fight-or-flight response kicks in. Deep breathing exercises counteract this by activating the parasympathetic nervous system, which promotes relaxation (Maxwell, 2021). Controlled breathing is an effective tool for regaining composure, whether you're dealing with a tense meeting, an argument, or unexpected bad news.

Try to pause and focus on your breath when you're in an intense situation. Practice diaphragmatic or guided breathing exercises to calm your body and mind. This can lower your heart rate and reduce the release of stress hormones. This simple practice can be a great tool to prevent anxiety from escalating and overwhelming you.

Practicing deep breathing regularly, not just during stressful moments, can enhance your ability to manage your emotions when needed. By training your body through consistent deep breathing exercises, your body learns to switch from stress to calm over time.

THE BENEFITS OF DEEP BREATHING EXERCISES

Deep breathing exercises have numerous health benefits that have been proven by science. By making it a habit, you can help lower your blood pressure, slow your heart rate, and maintain the correct levels of oxygen and carbon dioxide in your blood. It can also reduce stress hormones and make you feel more relaxed (Seppälä et al., 2020).

Deep breathing activates the parasympathetic nervous system, responsible for the "rest and digest" functions in the body, counteracting the "fight or flight" response induced by stress. Deliberately controlling your breath can influence your body's automatic functions, promoting relaxation and emotional stability.

Practical Tips for Daily Integration

If you're new to practicing deep breathing techniques, here are a few guidelines to help you:

- Morning ritual: Start your day with intention by practicing deep breathing as soon as you wake up. Before reaching for your phone or jumping into your to-do list, take 2-3 minutes to focus on slow, deep breaths. This will set a calm and centered tone for the day ahead.
- During commutes: Use your commute as an opportunity to practice deep breathing. Whether driving, taking public transportation, or walking, you can take slow, deep breaths to release tension and prepare for the day ahead or unwind after a long one.
- Breathing breaks at work: Instead of mindlessly scrolling through your phone during short breaks, dedicate a few moments to deep breathing. Try setting a timer every hour to remind yourself to take a "breathing break." Even just one minute of focused deep breathing can help reduce stress and restore focus.
- Pre-meal mindfulness: Before eating, take a few deep breaths to relax your body and mind. This practice not only helps with emotional regulation but can also improve digestion by reducing stress before meals.
- Pair with physical activity: Incorporate deep breathing into your exercise routine, whether it's yoga, stretching, or a post-workout cooldown. Focus on breathing deeply during stretches or while cooling down to enhance relaxation and recovery.
- Bedtime wind-down: As part of your nightly routine, use deep breathing to unwind before bed. To signal your body that it's time to relax, lay in bed, take slow breaths, and focus on long exhales. This practice helps calm the mind and prepare you for restful sleep.

Integrating deep breathing into these small moments throughout the day becomes a natural and effortless part of your routine, helping you maintain emotional balance and mental clarity.

PROGRESSIVE MUSCLE RELAXATION (PMR)

PMR is a highly effective technique for improving emotional regulation and managing stress. This relaxation technique involves systematically tensing and relaxing different muscle groups in the body, offering immediate relief from physical tension and emotional stress.

The first step in practicing PMR is identifying specific muscle groups to work on. You can begin from either end of your body, starting from your toes and working your way up, or starting at your head and working your way down. The key is to focus on one small muscle group at a time, such as your toes, calves, thighs, buttocks, abdomen, hands, arms, shoulders, neck, jaw, and forehead.

Here's a step-by-step guide to practicing PMR:

- Find a quiet and comfortable place where you won't be disturbed. Lying down is often recommended for effective results. However, you can also do it while sitting at a desk or even in a car.
- Close your eyes to block out any distractions, and take a few deep breaths to slow your heart rate, calm your mind, and relax your body.
- Next, take a deep breath while contracting the muscles in the target area, and hold this tension for about five seconds.
- Pay attention to how the tension feels; this will help you distinguish between a tense and relaxed muscle.
- After holding the contraction, slowly exhale and release the tension in the muscle group for five to ten seconds. Visualize the muscle becoming loose and relaxed, and notice any sensations of relief or lightness.
- Repeat these steps with each muscle group as you progress through your body.

THE BENEFITS OF PMR

Like other relaxation techniques, practicing PMR has physical and mental health benefits. Practicing PMR techniques:

- **Activates the body's sympathetic nervous system:** When stressed, your heart rate increases and you experience tense muscles. Practicing PMR allows your body to switch to rest and digest mode, which lowers your heart rate and blood pressure, calming the body and mind.
- **Trains your body to recognize and respond to signs of stress more effectively:** With time, you'll identify early signals of muscle tension and can use PMR to alleviate it before it escalates. This reduces chronic stress and promotes a sense of control over your emotional and physical well-being.
- **Can help you deal with intense stress:** For instance, a short PMR session targeting specific muscle groups can provide fast relief if you're nervous before a major work presentation or feeling overwhelmed because you can't find your keys. While a full-body PMR session can take around 10 to 20 minutes, focusing on just one area can offer quick comfort in just a few minutes.

Pairing PMR with other relaxation techniques can make it even more effective in reducing stress. Practices like deep breathing, visualization, and mindfulness meditation work well alongside PMR. For example, you can incorporate deep breathing into your PMR routine by taking slow, deep breaths while tensing and relaxing your muscles. Visualization is another helpful technique. Imagine a peaceful scene or positive outcome to enhance the relaxation experience when practicing PMR. Mindfulness meditation is also a great addition. When you focus on the present moment, you fully engage with your bodily sensations. Combining these techniques can lead to a more powerful and comprehensive stress-relief experience.

EMOTIONAL JOURNALING

Emotional regulation is an essential skill for managing your emotions and actions effectively. One way to improve your emotional regulation is practicing emotional journaling. Emotional journaling involves recording and reflecting on your feelings, significantly enhancing your self-awareness and improving your mental and emotional health.

THE BENEFITS OF EMOTIONAL JOURNALING

Regularly recording and reflecting on your emotions can improve self-awareness. When you take the time to write about your feelings, you become more attuned to your emotions. This practice gives you a sense of clarity in your thoughts, providing a clearer picture of your internal world. You will start noticing your behavioral patterns and triggers by consistently documenting your feelings. For example, you may witness certain situations or people always making you feel a certain way, like stressed or happy. Recognizing these patterns empowers you to anticipate and manage your reactions more effectively.

Emotional journaling can be a valuable tool for processing complex emotions. Life often throws us into situations that make us feel all sorts of emotions, some of which can be pretty confusing. Writing about these feelings can be a great way to assess and understand what's going on. It allows you to explore why you feel a certain way and the underlying causes. For example, if you feel anxious about an upcoming event, writing about it can uncover the root cause of your anxiety. It could be the fear of failure, uncertainty, or past experiences. Either way, writing about your emotions can help you make sense of them and find strategies to cope in the future.

Emotions are energy in motion; bottling them up inside leads to stress, anxiety, and even physical ailments. Journaling serves as an emotional outlet to release these pent-up emotions. It acts as a therapeutic exercise where you can freely express your thoughts and feelings without judgment, facilitating emotional healing. This release can be incredibly cathartic, lightening the emotional load and promoting a sense of relief.

Studies show that expressive journaling can reduce stress levels and alleviate symptoms of anxiety and depression (*The Power of Journaling for Well-Being: A Path to Self-Discovery and Healing*, 2023). Journaling prevents you from getting stuck in a loop of negative thoughts by giving you a structured way to address those thoughts. Instead of constantly worrying, journaling offers a safe space to reflect on your feelings in a healthier way.

Additionally, emotional journaling can improve your mood and overall outlook on life. You develop a more positive perspective by getting in touch with your emotions and recognizing your progress over time. Over time, you will likely notice growth in your emotional resilience and ability to handle challenging situations.

CARRYING OUT YOUR JOURNALING PROCESS

Using structured journaling with prompts can guide your journaling practice. Prompts are questions or statements that spark reflection and guide your writing. They can be helpful when you feel stuck or need help with what to write about. Some prompts are simple questions, like asking yourself how you feel in the moment. In contrast, others are more in-depth and encourage you to explore the underlying causes of your emotions, for example, asking yourself, *What past experiences influence my current emotions?* Using prompts like these can help uncover hidden thoughts and feelings you may not realize were there.

Creating a routine can make your journaling practice much more effortless when taking the first step. Set aside time each day or week for your journaling practice; it will become a habit over time. Whether you do it in the morning or at night, having a consistent slot helps you prioritize this valuable self-care practice. Dedicating 15-20 minutes per session can positively impact your emotional well-being.

Sharing your journaling experience with a trusted friend or therapist can also be helpful. Sharing your thoughts and reflections with someone else can offer new perspectives and validation. It allows you to process your emotions in dialogue, adding another layer of understanding and support.

Remember, emotional journaling aims not to judge or criticize yourself but to explore and understand your emotions better. Be kind and compassionate toward yourself during this process. Acknowledge your feelings without labeling them as good or bad. Every emotion has a place and serves a purpose in your overall emotional health.

KEY TAKEAWAYS

As you work through the process of overcoming toxic behaviors, it's essential to recognize that healing is a journey that requires patience, self-compassion, and consistent practice. Cultivating emotional balance through intentional breathwork, mindful connection to your body, and emotional journaling can be transformative.

Practicing deep breathing techniques can significantly enhance your emotional regulation. Progressive muscle relaxation helps you tune into your body's signals, reminding you that emotions are often stored physically. By learning to release tension, you can let go of emotional buildup, creating more space for balance and clarity in your interactions with others. Emotional journaling, on the other hand, serves as an emotional outlet. It allows you to pour unprocessed thoughts and feelings onto paper, offering a safe space to explore your deeper truths without judgment. By expressing your emotions this way, you gain insight into the root causes of your behaviors and patterns.

As you work on yourself, remember that overcoming toxic behavior is not just about breaking bad habits; it's about nurturing healthier, more compassionate ways of being. Breathwork, body awareness, and journaling are more than coping tools; they are gateways to transformation. They invite you to cultivate mindfulness, regulate your emotions, and connect deeply with yourself and others. By consistently practicing these techniques, you will notice shifts in how you react to stress and relate to others.

As you move forward, remember that real change comes from within. These practices are meant to support your journey, helping you replace toxic behaviors with emotional intelligence, empathy, and compassion for yourself and others. Embrace these tools as part of your daily routine, and trust that with each breath, movement, and written word, you are laying the foundation for lasting emotional balance.

CHAPTER 7
RELATIONSHIP SKILLS

Healthy relationships require effort, understanding, and respect.

UNKNOWN

Effective negotiation is a cornerstone of healthy relationships. At its core, negotiation is about finding a balance between your needs and other people's needs. This means practicing compromise and understanding that it's not always about "winning" but creating outcomes that benefit everyone involved.

Building healthy relationships requires effort, understanding, and respect. It requires consciously improving skills that promote better communication, conflict resolution, and mutual respect. Without these foundational skills, relationships can become strained, leading to misunderstandings and unresolved conflicts. To nurture healthy relationships, you must learn and apply practical relationship skills that promote peace.

NEGOTIATION SKILLS

Conflicts are inevitable in relationships. However, learning and applying negotiation skills can transform potentially toxic exchanges into opportunities for resolution and growth.

Successful negotiations depend on your ability to see things from different viewpoints, which paves the way to finding solutions that benefit everyone involved and effective conflict resolution.

Below are a couple of strategies you can use to improve your negotiation skills:

PRACTICE ACTIVE LISTENING

Active listening is a crucial part of any negotiation process. It's more than just hearing what someone is saying; it's about understanding their viewpoint and how they feel. This eases tensions, breaks stalemates, and helps you gather important information.

Active listening involves paraphrasing what the other person said, asking for clarity where you don't understand, and acknowledging their feelings and concerns. This approach ensures that everyone feels heard and validated, which is vital for building trust and finding common ground.

USE NEGOTIATION TECHNIQUES TO RESOLVE CONFLICTS

Effective negotiation requires using a set of skills to help you communicate and resolve conflicts amicably. When negotiating, aim for a win-win outcome where everyone feels heard. One helpful technique is looking for hidden satisfiers that may not be immediately apparent but could significantly influence the outcome if properly addressed.

Picture a couple, Jill and Tom, discussing how they want to spend their weekends. Jill likes to stay in and unwind, while Tom prefers going out to discover new things. At first glance, they have different preferences on how they want to spend their free time. However, there might be deeper reasons behind their desires:

- **Jill (likes staying home):** Her hidden satisfier might be wanting to have some alone time with her partner, where they can genuinely connect emotionally. Even though she says she wants to relax, what she really craves is

undisturbed, close time with Tom to strengthen their bond.
- **Tom (wants to go out):** His hidden satisfier could be a desire for shared experiences and adventure. While he suggests going out, what he may truly need is to bond through new activities, reinforcing the excitement and novelty in the relationship.

Finally, Jill and Tom agree to compromise by alternating between quiet, at-home weekends and outdoor activities that cultivate emotional connection and shared adventure.

Open communication can uncover underlying factors in a relationship. By addressing the needs behind someone's initial request, you can find a resolution that satisfies both of you, even if it requires compromise. Understanding and addressing hidden satisfiers can lead to greater satisfaction, allowing everyone to feel valued and understood, ultimately strengthening the relationship.

THE BENEFITS OF EFFECTIVE NEGOTIATION

Effective negotiation is essential to resolving conflicts constructively and encouraging people to work together. Learning to negotiate and resolve disputes amicably is crucial for building better relationships.

Learning and applying these strategies in everyday interactions can significantly improve your relationships. Practicing active listening and finding compromise can improve your negotiation skills. By focusing on understanding and resolving your differences, you can create healthier, more positive relationships without getting stuck in the same negative patterns.

DEVELOPING NEGOTIATION SKILLS

Role-playing scenarios are an effective strategy to practice negotiation skills. You can test different ways of approaching a situation, see what works and what doesn't, and get better at negotiating without the stress of real-life consequences. Role-playing is a safe space to learn and improve your communication skills. By simulating real-life interactions, you can practice healthier responses, develop emotional awareness, and think quickly when faced with conflict.

To make the most of this practice, find someone to keep you accountable. For example, if you tend to become defensive in arguments, role-playing a disagreement with a trusted friend can help you practice staying calm, listening actively, and responding constructively. This allows you to break old patterns and replace them with positive habits in a controlled setting. An accountability partner can provide honest feedback and help you reflect on areas for improvement.

It's crucial to seek feedback during practice sessions. Constructive feedback can help you fine-tune your negotiation techniques, enhance your approach, and become a more skilled negotiator.

LISTENING TO FEEDBACK

One of the most powerful ways to achieve personal growth is to seek feedback from others. Outside perspectives provide invaluable insights you may overlook, whether it's feedback on your communication style, behavior, or decision-making. When requesting feedback, choose people whose opinions you trust and respect, and make it clear that you're open to constructive criticism.

Listening to feedback requires more than just hearing it; it means accepting it without becoming defensive. Instead of reacting to feedback as an attack, view it as an opportunity to improve the way you communicate and strengthen your relationships.

THE BENEFITS OF SEEKING FEEDBACK

Seeking feedback from others about your behavior and communication style can help you understand how others perceive you. It's more than simply asking whether someone liked or disliked what you did; it involves seeking specific insights into areas you need to improve on. For instance, you can ask your colleagues how your communication style affects team meetings or check in with your friends to see how your responses during conflicts make them feel. The idea is to get honest and constructive criticism that gives you a different perspective of yourself.

Once you've received feedback, the next step is to listen actively without getting defensive. This involves more than hearing words; it's about connecting with the person giving feedback, showing empathy, and that you value their input. For example, instead of immediately defending yourself when you receive criticism, take a moment to process what was said. You could respond with, "I understand why you felt that way," or "Thank you for pointing that out."

Active listening opens the door to valuable insights you might otherwise miss if you are defensive. Remember, the purpose of feedback is not to attack but to help you grow.

APPLYING FEEDBACK

After receiving feedback:

- **Spend time reflecting on it:** Consider whether or not the points raised are valid and if they resonate with how you perceive yourself. You can carry out this reflective process through journaling, talking to someone you trust, or just quietly thinking about what was said. Suppose a colleague suggests that you often interrupt others during conversations. Think back on times when this might have happened and the possible reasons behind this habit. Understanding the root cause of such behaviors can help you develop an effective action plan.
- **Create a plan to address any areas that need improvement:** For example, if someone suggests that you need to work on your listening skills, your action plan could involve practicing active listening skills like summarizing what others say before responding or asking for clarification. Set specific goals and timelines and identify your needed resources, such as attending a communication workshop or reading relevant books and articles. This approach ensures

that you acknowledge feedback and translate it into noticeable changes.
- **Keep track of how you're doing after receiving feedback:** Check in now and then with the people who gave you the advice to see if they notice any improvement in the areas highlighted. This shows your commitment to change and allows you to get further guidance to make any adjustments. For instance, you could ask a friend or your partner, "Do you think I've been handling disagreements better?" Their feedback can encourage you to keep moving in the right direction.

Understanding the importance of listening to feedback is essential for personal growth and maintaining positive relationships. By actively seeking feedback, you develop self-awareness and recognize areas where you can improve. This can help you to address any blind spots in your behavior or attitudes that you may not have realized were affecting those around you. Additionally, receiving feedback from others can give you valuable insight into patterns or trends you might have yet to notice on your own. When you are willing to make changes based on others' input, you show that you value and respect their opinions.

Additionally, accepting feedback gracefully can make you more approachable and trustworthy. People will likely perceive you as someone committed to personal growth and maintaining harmonious relationships. This encourages a culture of open communication, where you view feedback as a way to improve yourself.

For example, if a co-worker tells you that your emails sometimes come off as a bit harsh. Instead of getting defensive, try to listen to what they're saying and think about how you can change your approach. You can start adding a friendly greeting or closing to your emails to soften the tone. After making some adjustments, follow up with the person to see if they've noticed any improvement. Taking these steps can help you track your progress and reinforce the positive changes you've made due to their feedback.

BUILDING TRUST

Trust is the core of any healthy relationship. Whether it's a friendship, romantic partnership, or professional connection, trust enables open communication, emotional safety, and long-term stability. Building trust and cultivating a sense of security in relationships requires:

- **Honesty and reliability:** When you are honest, you create an atmosphere where transparency thrives, making it easier to address concerns and avoid misunderstandings. On the other hand, reliability reinforces trust by demonstrating consistency in your actions, showing that people can count on you in both good times and challenging moments. Together, these qualities lay a strong foundation for lasting connections. When people know they can rely on you, it creates a safe space for openness and vulnerability, allowing relationships to flourish.
- **Consistency and dependability:** Being consistent means that people can count on you to follow through on your promises and be there for them when they need you. For instance, if you promise to spend time together or support your partner during difficult times, doing what you said you would do helps build trust. Aligning your actions with your words shows that you are trustworthy.
- **Open and honest communication:** Transparency creates a comfortable environment where everyone can freely communicate their thoughts and feelings. This means not only expressing your needs and concerns but also listening to what others have to say without criticizing them. Open and honest conversations lead to a better understanding of other's perspectives. Whether you're talking about your day, making plans for the future, or sharing your concerns, being open and honest with each other can help you build trust in your relationships.
- **Addressing and resolving conflicts transparently:** Conflicts are bound to happen, but how you deal with

them can significantly impact the outcome. Approaching disagreements with empathy and a willingness to see things from others' perspectives can help you resolve conflicts amicably. Rather than point fingers and get defensive, focus on finding a solution that works for everyone. Avoiding personal attacks and staying focused on the problem at hand can lead to a more positive resolution. For example, if you disagree on how to handle finances with your partner, it's important to talk things out and find a middle ground instead of ignoring the issue. Transparency in handling conflicts shows that you and your partner value the relationship enough to work through challenging problems together.

- **Practicing active listening and expressing your thoughts clearly:** When interacting with someone, give them your full attention, acknowledge their feelings, and respond thoughtfully. For instance, try to eliminate distractions like phones during conversations and make eye contact to show that you are genuinely engaged in the discussion. In return, share your thoughts honestly, whether about a concern, a plan, or just how your day went. This mutual openness deepens your trust.
- **Respectful communication:** When conflicts arise, communicate your feelings without resorting to hurtful language. It's essential to focus on the issue rather than placing blame. For instance, using "I" statements such as "I feel upset when..." instead of "You always..." helps you express your feelings without sounding like you're accusing them. Listening to someone's perspective and working together to find a resolution shows that you prioritize the relationship.
- **Patience and consistency in your actions:** Building trust takes patience and consistent effort. Trust isn't built overnight; it's a continuous process of small yet significant actions. Each sincere gesture, honest conversation, and resolved conflict adds to the overall trust in the relationship.

For example, regularly checking in with loved ones about how things are going or planning activities together can strengthen your bond. Over time, these practices solidify your trust, creating supportive relationships.

- **Transparency in all aspects of your relationships:** This promotes authenticity. Being open about your intentions, feelings, and actions is crucial to building trust and ensuring no hidden agendas. For example, if you're experiencing stress at work, sharing this with your partner helps them understand what you're going through and allows you to support each other. Keeping secrets or withholding important information can damage trust, while transparency lays the groundwork for a trusting relationship.

Building trust in a relationship strengthens your connections and is good for your overall well-being. Knowing that there is someone who will support, understand, and stand by you brings a sense of hope and emotional comfort. This sense of security allows you to thrive personally and within the relationship. For example, knowing your partner is trustworthy gives you the confidence to try new things and take risks because you know they have your back.

Finally, it's essential to recognize and celebrate milestones in your relationships. Showing appreciation for each other's efforts in building trust can go a long way in creating a positive dynamic. For example, taking time to express gratitude for the support you receive and reflecting on the journey of trust-building can create lasting memories and deepen your connections. These small gestures can reinforce the trust and love you have for each other in a meaningful way.

KEY TAKEAWAYS

Building healthy relationships takes work, compassion, and mutual respect. Improving your negotiation skills can significantly impact your relationships. Listening to others, using smart negotiation strategies, and being open to feedback can help you solve problems peacefully and create a strong foundation of trust. These approaches can improve your communication and ability to work together more effectively, creating a positive atmosphere where everyone feels valued and understood.

Mastering negotiation can significantly improve the quality of your relationships. These tools empower you to handle conflicts with empathy, resolve issues more effectively, and cultivate deeper connections with others. By honing your ability to negotiate thoughtfully, listen with intention, and nurture trust, you create a foundation for stronger, more adaptable relationships based on mutual respect and understanding.

Integrating these practices into your daily life will enhance your connections and experience more fulfilling, harmonious, and meaningful interactions. Ultimately, these skills are the cornerstone of healthier relationships that thrive on collaboration and open communication.

CHAPTER 8
POSITIVE REINFORCEMENT

Reinforcement is the key to reinforcing positive behavior.

UNKNOWN

Behavioral change requires self-awareness, commitment, and patience. Positive reinforcement is one of the most powerful tools in this process. Celebrating even small victories encourages you to keep working on yourself. Think for a moment—when was the last time you truly rewarded yourself for reaching a significant milestone? Whether it's treating yourself to something you love, taking a well-deserved break, or simply acknowledging your hard work, self-recognition can be the battery you need to keep pushing you forward.

Positive reinforcement shifts your mindset from focusing on the struggles of change to appreciating your progress, making the journey more enjoyable and sustainable. By rewarding your efforts, you not only boost your confidence but also reinforce the belief that growth is achievable, creating a lasting impact on your overall development.

Rewarding yourself for your efforts creates a feedback loop of success, reinforcing the positive behaviors that led to your achievements. When you recognize and celebrate your progress, your brain associates those behaviors with positive emotions, making it more likely that you'll repeat them in the future. However, positive reinforcement is not just about rewards; it's about reshaping your mindset and celebrating progress. Too often, people focus on what's wrong and what needs to be fixed or avoided. But the power of positive reinforcement lies in shifting that focus. Instead of fixing your mind on your mistakes or setbacks, it helps you acknowledge the changes you're making and encourages you to continue down the path of growth. The more you reward yourself for healthy behavior, the more likely you are to continue practicing it. These small celebrations of progress can profoundly impact your self-esteem, motivation, and overall growth.

CELEBRATING MILESTONES

Recognizing your achievements promotes positive reinforcement and encourages you to keep developing positive habits. Celebrating your successes, no matter how small, can motivate you to stay on the path of personal growth. It solidifies your progress and affirms that you are moving forward, even on days when change feels slow.

By appreciating your efforts, you create a positive reinforcement loop. Remember, celebrations aren't just about the end goal; they are about recognizing the steps along the way. Whether you've overcome a toxic habit, established a healthier boundary, or handled an emotional trigger in a new way, each achievement is a testament to your commitment to personal growth.

ACKNOWLEDGING EVERY STEP FORWARD

Recognizing and appreciating the effort you put into achieving your goals is just as important as celebrating the result. By acknowledging the hard work and determination that goes into the process, you stay motivated to continue pushing forward even when you haven't reached your final goal. For example, if you're overcoming toxic jealousy in relationships and notice its first signs, but instead of reacting impulsively, you calmly communicate your feelings, this moment is a milestone worth celebrating. While you may not have completely eradicated the jealousy, you've taken a massive step in controlling your response. Recognizing this small victory, whether by writing about it in a journal or treating yourself to a favorite activity, helps reinforce the behavior change and motivates you to continue improving, even though you haven't yet reached the final goal of fully managing your jealousy. Each milestone, whether it's catching yourself before acting on toxic impulses or celebrating how you responded calmly in the face of an argument, is a critical part of the transformation journey.

SHARE YOUR SUCCESSES

Celebrating in isolation can feel limited. When you share your successes with friends, family, or even a support group, you open the door for encouragement and support from others. People who care about you will help elevate your success by celebrating with you, offering encouragement, and reminding you of how far you've come. These shared moments nurture connection and amplify your sense of accomplishment.

SET REWARDS FOR YOUR ACCOMPLISHMENTS

Setting personal rewards for accomplishing goals is a great way to stay motivated. Everyone's rewards will be different, and that's okay. Choosing something you value and are excited to work toward is important. This could be something physical like buying yourself a treat or taking a day off, or something more personal like spending time doing something you love or seeking new opportunities for personal growth. The main idea is to give yourself something to look forward to and appreciate yourself for all your hard work.

THE BENEFITS OF CELEBRATING MILESTONES

Celebrating success isn't just about feeling good at the moment; it comes with lasting benefits that fuel long-term personal growth and transformation beyond momentary satisfaction. As you create a foundation for sustained change, you'll experience the following benefits:

- **Motivation to continue on your growth journey:** Celebrating milestones injects new energy into your journey. Each time you recognize an achievement, you experience a psychological lift, a surge of positive emotion that creates a mental reward system that makes you eager to continue (Amabile and Kramer, 2011). By pausing to celebrate, you signal to yourself that your work is valuable and the journey is worth it. This increased motivation sustains you during challenging times when you feel overwhelmed and helps you stay committed to your long-term goals.
- **Positive reinforcement:** Celebrating milestones is a form of positive reinforcement that strengthens the behaviors that led to those victories. When you acknowledge your progress, you are more likely to repeat the actions and choices that contributed to it. The positive emotions linked to success reinforce the neural pathways associated with those behaviors, making them easier to practice over time (McNally, 2024). Whether it's resisting a toxic impulse or responding with empathy instead of defensiveness, celebrating positive behaviors cements them as habits. Over time, this makes healthier responses more automatic, enabling you to replace old, toxic behaviors with constructive ones.
- **Continued effort and growth:** Success breeds success. Celebrating milestones helps build momentum, giving you the confidence and energy to keep pushing forward, even when the path becomes difficult. You're continually reminded that growth is happening. As you experience the benefits of your progress, it becomes easier to envision the larger transformation you're working toward. The cumulative effect of celebrating achievements is that it creates a positive outlook on the journey itself. It reinforces the belief that change is possible. This fuels your resilience and keeps you on track, especially during periods when progress seems slow.

Celebrations aren't just gratification; they are strategic tools that motivate you, establish positive behaviors, and fuel continued growth. By making celebration a regular part of your journey, you create a cycle of positivity, cultivating the mindset necessary for lasting change.

REWARDING POSITIVE BEHAVIOR

Rewarding yourself for positive behavior is an effective way to sustain change. Setting up a reward system gives you something to look forward to, making the hard work feel worthwhile. The rewards don't need to be extravagant—they just need to be meaningful and tailored to your personal preferences.

Here's how you can create your personalized reward system for good behavior:

- **Tailor your reward system to your needs and goals:** This means choosing rewards that matter to you personally. To illustrate, let's say your goal is to overcome toxic communication patterns, like being overly critical or using passive-aggressive language during arguments. After practicing healthy communication by calmly and respectfully expressing yourself in a tough conversation, you might celebrate this milestone in a way that personally motivates you. If you value self-care, you could schedule a relaxing activity like a massage or engage in your favorite activity. Or, if you enjoy socializing, why not treat yourself to a night out with friends or a special dinner with a loved one, sharing your progress and celebrating the improvement together?
- **Set rewarding incentives:** The reward should bring you undeniable pleasure and satisfaction, making you more likely to keep up the good behavior. Research shows intrinsic motivation is key to habit formation (Judah et al., 2018). Choosing rewards that align with your interests and passions can make the journey fun and worthy. For instance,

if you love reading, you might feel thrilled to earn a new book for staying consistent with your habit.
- **Keep track of your progress:** By keeping records of your achievements, you can see how far you've come and the effectiveness of your rewards. You can do this in different ways, such as journaling, using apps, or using visual aids like charts to track your progress. Reviewing these records regularly helps you understand what motivates you the most and adjust your rewards accordingly.
- **Adjust your rewards based on their effectiveness:** What might make you happy at first may change over time, so it's important to be flexible and adaptable. If a reward that used to make you happy doesn't do the trick anymore, trying something new can bring back that spark. For example, if you're getting bored of going out to eat all the time, maybe trying something fun and different, like going to a concert or a cooking class, could be more exciting.

Celebrating small victories encourages continued effort and growth. Recognizing and rewarding yourself for even minor achievements keeps the momentum and process enjoyable. Small victories give you a sense of accomplishment and reinforce positive behavior, making it easier to tackle more significant goals.

When setting personal rewards for your achievements, be specific. Clearly outlining the requirements for earning a reward makes the process more objective. For example, to overcome toxic anger outbursts, you might set clear, specific goals for managing your emotions in difficult situations.

An outlined requirement could be: "For the next week, if I feel anger rising, I will practice deep breathing for 5 minutes before responding to any conversation. If I succeed in doing this in three different situations, I will reward myself with a night out or a favorite self-care activity." Clearly defining your goal and practicing calming techniques before reacting creates a fair and measurable process for earning your reward. This structure ensures you know exactly what is required, making it easier to track your progress objectively. Achieving the outlined goal makes the reward feel genuinely earned and builds confidence.

Sharing your accomplishments with the people you care about increases the positive impact of the reward system. Getting recognized by your friends and family gives you that extra boost of emotional support and validation. Celebrating your achievements with others creates a supportive atmosphere that motivates you to keep working on yourself. You can share your progress by posting updates on social media, having a small get-together to mark milestones, or just discussing your goals and successes with the people around you.

TRACKING YOUR PROGRESS

Keeping track of your progress is vital to making positive changes in your life. Monitoring your journey can help you identify what's working and what's not, allowing you to adapt your strategies accordingly. To track your progress, you could:

- **Keep a journal:** As discussed in Chapter 1, journaling is crucial to your growth journey. It helps you reflect and keep track of your progress. Whether you like to write in a notebook or use a digital journaling app, consistency is key. Recording your daily or weekly wins and challenges creates a clear picture of your efforts and results. Additionally, reflecting on your actions and outcomes can help you stay focused and motivated to keep pushing toward your goals.
- **Set SMART goals:** Setting measurable goals and milestones is essential to tracking your progress effectively. Your goals should be specific, attainable, relevant, and time-bound. By breaking down objectives into smaller, manageable milestones, you create a roadmap that guides your efforts and keeps you focused. Each milestone acts as a checkpoint, providing opportunities to celebrate small victories and reassess your strategies. For example, if your goal is to improve your communication skills at work, a measurable milestone could be giving a successful

presentation at the next team meeting in two weeks. Documenting these goals and milestones in your journal ensures clear targets and a structured plan.
- **Review and analyze your progress regularly:** Reviewing your progress from time to time can help you understand where you stand and where you need to make adjustments. Set aside time each week or month to review your journal entries and evaluate your progress. This review process can help you identify areas for growth and any obstacles that may impede your progress. For instance, if you're consistently struggling to reach a goal, it could be a sign that you need a different approach or additional resources. Analyzing your progress can help you identify what's working and what's not. This will help you make smarter decisions and stay focused on your objectives.

Adjusting your strategies based on your results is the final piece of the puzzle. As you review your progress and identify areas of improvement, it's crucial to tweak your plans accordingly. Flexibility and adaptability are vital to optimizing your outcomes. Try a different approach if a specific strategy isn't working out as you hoped. For instance, if rewarding yourself with a small reward for achieving a goal isn't motivating enough, consider increasing the reward's value or rewarding yourself differently. Your journaling entries will give you valuable insights on where to adjust your approach. Continuously refining your strategies ensures that you remain aligned with your goals and enhance your chances of success.

KEY TAKEAWAYS

Positive reinforcement encourages positive behaviors. Rewarding yourself for your progress, however small, not only motivates you to keep moving forward but also reinforces healthy actions that contribute to lasting change. This approach shifts your focus from self-criticism and guilt to encouragement and self-empowerment, creating a supportive environment for personal growth.

Celebrating small victories cultivates a sense of accomplishment, making it easier to build new, positive habits. As you acknowledge each step forward, you're more likely to continue pushing toward larger goals, transforming toxic behaviors into constructive patterns that support healthier relationships and emotional well-being.

Positive reinforcement helps you stay committed, motivated, and resilient as you evolve into a better version of yourself. By integrating rewards into your healing process, you create a sustainable path to growth—one built on self-compassion, perseverance, and continued effort.

CHAPTER 9
SOCIAL SKILLS

Social skills are the tools to connect, communicate, and collaborate effectively.

UNKNOWN

Imagine this: You're at a social gathering, trying your best to make a good impression. You know the drill—smile, make eye contact, and say something charming. Except, every time you try to jump into a conversation, you either interrupt someone mid-sentence or say something awkward like, "So... you guys believe in aliens, right?" The group politely chuckles, but their eyes say, "Who invited this person?"

Many of us struggle with toxic social behaviors and don't even realize how these habits are affecting our relationships. Social gatherings become a minefield of discomfort, not because of a lack of desire to connect but because toxic tendencies like over-talking, being overly critical, or failing to read the room can push people away rather than draw them in. Until you decide to reflect and actively work on your social skills, navigating social situations will feel like walking a tightrope, one misstep, and you're plunging into a pool of awkwardness.

Developing social skills is fundamental to building effective connections and achieving fruitful interactions. Social skills like being friendly, listening well, and knowing how to act in different social situations can help you easily engage in meaningful conversations.

Social skills aren't something we're born with. You don't have to be the life of the party to master social skills, but you can definitely leave the party with fewer awkward conversations and more genuine connections.

THE ROLE OF NETWORKING IN BUILDING SOCIAL SKILLS

Networking is essential for building and improving your social skills, personally and professionally. Meeting new people and interacting with different social groups teaches you how to be more comfortable in unfamiliar situations. This can enhance your confidence and help you improve your communication and relationship-building skills.

Entering new social groups can feel intimidating at first. However, it's in these situations that you learn and develop your social skills. Each interaction gives you an opportunity to improve how you communicate, listen, and connect with others. Attending events like conferences, community get-togethers, or casual meet-ups are great opportunities to practice these skills. For example, introducing yourself to someone you don't know at a networking event can be a great way to practice first impressions—a crucial aspect of social interaction. Over time, as you encounter different personalities and conversation styles, you become more adept at handling diverse social situations quickly and confidently.

THE BENEFITS OF NETWORKING

Networking is not just about expanding your contacts; it is a great way to refine your social skills. By consistently interacting with new people, you can practice conversation techniques, body language, and other interpersonal skills to improve your overall social interactions. Let's look at a few benefits of building connections through networking.

- Networking is crucial in today's job market. By meeting like-minded people, you can discover new career paths, find people to collaborate with, and get guidance from mentors. Did you know that most job openings aren't even advertised? About 80% of jobs are filled through connections made through networking (Lopez, 2023). This shows how important networking is when looking for job opportunities and advancing your career. When you connect with others in your field, you become part of a community where news about job openings, business ventures, and industry developments is shared. Additionally, talking with seasoned professionals can give you valuable insights and direction for your career journey.

- On a personal level, networking can help build friendships and support systems. Sharing experiences and mutual interests can deepen connections, evolving into lasting friendships. These relationships can provide emotional support during challenging times, celebrate your successes, and offer different perspectives on various life situations. Networking extends your support system beyond your immediate circle, enriching your personal life.
- Networking provides continuous opportunities to interact and enhance your social skills. Regularly attending networking events or social gatherings pushes you out of your comfort zone and encourages you to meet new people. This constant exposure hones your communication skills, making you more articulate and effective in conveying your ideas. Additionally, it improves your listening skills—an integral part of effective communication. Paying attention to what others say, asking insightful questions, and showing genuine interest in their responses cultivate trust and respect in your relationships. As your communication skills improve, so does your ability to collaborate and work efficiently with others.
- Effective networking can expand your social circle. Meeting people from varied backgrounds, professions, and cultures broadens your worldview and introduces you to new ideas and ways of thinking. For instance, connecting with

someone from a different industry might expose you to alternative problem-solving techniques or innovative approaches you can apply in your field. This diversity of thought enhances your professional knowledge and promotes empathy and cultural competence. Understanding and appreciating different viewpoints promotes inclusivity and creates a harmonious environment in both professional and social settings.
- Expanding your social circle through networking gives you access to more resources and opportunities. For example, joining professional associations, attending industry-specific events, or participating in online forums can introduce you to thought leaders and influencers who can provide valuable advice and mentorship. Being part of such networks also keeps you updated with the latest industry trends, best practices, and innovations, which are crucial for staying competitive in today's fast-paced professional landscape.

Successful social interactions in different environments require a clear strategy. Start by setting specific goals for each networking opportunity you attend. Whether you want to connect with a set number of new people, learn more about a particular topic, or find potential partners, having a plan will keep you on track. It's also helpful to have a brief introduction that quickly communicates who you are, what you're involved in, and your goals for the interaction. This introduction serves as an icebreaker and sets the tone for meaningful conversations.

When networking, make a real effort to engage with the people you meet. Ask them open-ended questions that require more than a yes or no answer, and pay attention to their responses. Not only will this show that you value their perspective, but it will also give you some valuable information and insights. Remember to follow up after your first meeting by email, social media, or setting up a casual coffee chat. This follow-up shows that you're serious about building a strong professional relationship.

It's also worthwhile to offer value to your connections. Networking is a two-way street; while you seek to gain from others, think about how you can contribute to their success. Share relevant information, offer assistance where possible, and connect them with others in your network who might benefit them. Adopting this reciprocal approach builds trust and strengthens your network, ensuring mutual growth and success.

BUILDING SOCIAL SKILLS THROUGH ROLE-PLAY

Role-playing is a great way to improve your social skills and ability to connect and communicate with others effectively. Engaging in role-play activities:

- **Create a safe space to make mistakes and learn from them without severe consequences:** For example, you could practice introducing yourself at a networking event, dealing with a disagreement at work, or handling a difficult conversation with a friend. Each scenario helps you build muscle memory and prepares you to respond more naturally and effectively when facing similar real-life situations.
- **Enhance your self-confidence:** Role-playing allows you to practice different social situations in a comfortable setting. This can prepare you for real-life interactions and build confidence. This newfound confidence isn't just limited to the moments practiced during role-play, but it can also positively impact all areas of communication.
- **Provide hands-on experience that you can't get from textbooks alone:** Whether doing it with a friend or a larger group, role-playing helps you actively get involved, stay engaged, and receive instant feedback. In personal situations, you can customize role-playing to tackle specific social challenges you may be dealing with. In group settings, it brings in different viewpoints and perspectives. This shared experience can be valuable because it reflects the diverse interactions you have in real life and helps you understand social dynamics better.

Seeking feedback on your performance in a role-playing session can help you identify what you did great and where you need to improve. Receiving constructive feedback can help you understand areas you need to work on without feeling discouraged. One way to do this is to have a structured debriefing session after the role-playing activity. This is a chance for everyone to share their thoughts and feelings on any issues that may have occurred. It's a great way to reflect and identify specific social skills you need to develop.

Role-playing goes beyond just helping you socialize better. It can help you understand how other people feel by allowing you to imagine what it's like to be in their shoes. This can help you build meaningful relationships. Additionally, role-playing can improve your problem-solving skills and creativity, as they often present challenges that require you to think on your feet, come up with solutions, and adapt to change—valuable skills for both professional and social set-ups. Role-playing is an ongoing process, and as you receive feedback, you can tweak your approach to be more effective.

THE ROLE OF FEEDBACK SESSIONS IN BUILDING SOCIAL SKILLS

In today's fast-paced social world, feedback sessions are a powerful way to improve social skills. They give you a chance to see yourself through the eyes of others, offering insights you might not notice on your own. In conversations or group settings, it's easy to get caught up in the moment and miss how your behaviors or words come across. That's where feedback comes in; it acts like a mirror, showing how others perceive your actions, words, and body language, helping you become more aware of how you connect with the people around you.

For example, say you have a habit of consistently interrupting others during meetings. You may only realize this habit once someone points it out in a feedback session. Once you're aware of this behavior, you can consciously improve, enhance your social skills, and contribute more effectively to team discussions.

Constructive criticism also plays a crucial role in improving and developing better social skills. Unlike negative criticism, which can demean and demotivate, constructive criticism aims to build up and guide you toward improvement. For instance, when someone says, "I appreciate your enthusiasm, but sometimes it comes across as overpowering. Could you try to allow others more time to speak?" instead of saying, "You are too aggressive in conversations," This type of feedback not only points out areas you need to improve on but also provides a pathway for positive change. The most helpful feedback is specific and actionable. Asking friends, family, or colleagues for feedback on your conversational style, body language, or tone of voice can provide insights you might otherwise overlook.

After receiving feedback, listening and actively applying the suggestions in your daily interactions is important. Start by identifying specific areas where you can make small, realistic changes, whether it's learning to be more patient, practicing empathy, or resisting the urge to dominate conversations. Once you've applied these adjustments, periodically check in with yourself or others to assess your progress. You can do this by reflecting on recent social interactions, asking for follow-up feedback, or even journaling about how certain situations went.

For example, in the case of our example above, if you've been told during a feedback session that you often interrupt others during conversations, making people feel dismissed. To work on this, you practice active listening by letting others finish their thoughts before responding. After a few weeks of consciously working on this, you might ask a trusted friend or colleague, "Hey, I've been trying to be a better listener. Have you noticed any difference?" This not only shows your commitment to growth but also gives you real-time updates on how well you're improving. The key is consistency and self-reflection. The more you keep this in mind, the more you will be able to replace toxic habits with healthier, more positive behaviors gradually.

KEY TAKEAWAYS

Building social skills is a transformative journey. It's about recognizing the impact of your actions, committing to change, and practicing healthier, more constructive ways to connect with others. While the process may feel challenging at times, every step, whether it's learning to listen, setting boundaries, or seeking feedback, brings you closer to more meaningful, respectful relationships.

Networking, role-playing, and feedback sessions can help you become more skilled at interacting with others in different situations. Networking lets you make connections that can help you grow personally and professionally. Role-playing is a fun way to practice talking to people and understanding their feelings. Feedback sessions can also provide advice on how to improve your social skills. Incorporating these practices into your daily life will help you easily handle different social situations. These tools empower you to break free from negative patterns and cultivate a supportive social environment where mutual respect and understanding thrive.

As you develop these skills, you'll improve your engagement with others and cultivate self-awareness, emotional intelligence, and empathy. These qualities are the foundation of genuine connection, allowing you to engage in more positive interactions in your personal and professional life.

Change takes time, but with effort and intention, you can move past old habits and build stronger, healthier social relationships that reflect your growth and commitment to a better version of yourself.

CHAPTER 10
STRESS MANAGEMENT

Stress is not what happens to us. It's our response to what happens. And response is something we can choose.

MAUREEN KILLORAN

Stress is that unwelcome guest who always seems to show up uninvited. Stress can sneak into your life and settle in, whether it's a tight work deadline, a challenging relationship, or even something as simple as rush-hour traffic. Imagine you're trying to unwind after a hectic day, and suddenly, you find yourself on the couch with the TV on, barely paying attention, eating leftover Chinese food at 1 a.m., and scrolling endlessly through social media. You think you're relaxing, but all you're doing is adding fuel to the fire of stress.

In these moments, we realize stress isn't something that goes away. It requires active management. The good news? With the right strategies, you can manage your stress levels.

Stress management is essential for leading a balanced and healthy life. Effectively managing stress can improve your emotional well-being and overall quality of life. Different stress-management techniques allow you to find personalized strategies that work best for you and fit your lifestyle. While some people may benefit from physical activities that elevate mood and provide a sense of control, others might find solace in eating nutritious food that energizes and promotes mental clarity. By trying different techniques, you will find effective ways to manage stress and build resilience and emotional stability.

EXERCISE AS AN EMOTIONAL OUTLET

Physical activity is one of the most effective ways to manage stress. Incorporating exercise into your daily routine can:

- **Enable your body to better cope with stress and its physiological effects:** Whether it's a morning jog, a yoga session, or a gym workout, physical activity is a natural stress reliever that promotes the release of endorphins, the body's feel-good hormones (Watson, 2021). Endorphins, often called "feel-good" hormones, are neurotransmitters that induce feelings of happiness and relaxation. This chemical reaction can significantly improve your emotional well-being and help combat the adverse effects of stress. For example, a brisk walk in the park or a vigorous session at the gym can leave you feeling more cheerful and less burdened by the worries of the day. This upbeat, uplifting mood does not just last for a moment; it can have long-lasting emotional benefits.
- **Enhance your overall physical health:** Exercise strengthens the cardiovascular system, improves lung function, and boosts immunity (Wong, 2024). For instance, regular aerobic exercises like swimming or bicycling improve cardiovascular health and give you a peaceful, almost meditative experience. These physical health benefits are essential because a healthy body can handle stress more efficiently.
- **Help you build healthy habits that support long-term stress relief:** By making exercise a regular part of your routine, you develop a habit that enhances your ability to manage stress. Over time, these activities become second nature, making it easier to cope with stress whenever it

arises. For example, attending a weekly yoga class or committing to a morning run can provide structure and a sense of control fundamental to reducing stress levels.

Finding the right kind of exercise that you enjoy is vital to making physical activity a lasting part of your life. Try out different activities until you find one that you genuinely enjoy, whether it's dancing, playing sports, hiking, or gardening. Having fun with your exercise routine will make it more likely that you'll stick with it and make it a regular part of your day.

When life gets busy and finding time for long workouts feels impossible, don't worry! Short bursts of exercise can still help you stay healthy. Even just taking a quick 10-minute walk during your lunch break or doing some stretches in the afternoon can make a huge difference. The key is to keep moving throughout the day. Try little things like using the stairs instead of the elevator, parking further away from your destination, or doing simple exercises at your desk.

Exercising with a friend or family member can motivate you and create a friendly competition. Having someone to chat with or cheer you on can make the entire experience much more enjoyable and create memories that strengthen the friendship. You can meet friends for walks, join a local sports team, or participate in group fitness classes. The social aspect of exercising together can provide emotional support, which can help you manage stress.

Try different physical activities, like strength training, cardio, and flexibility exercises, to keep your exercise routine fun and effective. For example, if you love running, try adding Pilates or yoga classes to improve flexibility and reduce muscle tightness. Mixing things up keeps things interesting and gives you a well-rounded approach to fitness and stress relief.

Keeping a positive attitude toward exercise is critical to reaping the benefits. Remember, it's not just something to check off your list. Instead, consider it an opportunity to relax, recharge, and look after yourself. Whether you enjoy a competitive sport or a peaceful walk in the park, find something you love and make it a regular part of your day.

THE ROLE OF NUTRITION IN MANAGING STRESS

In today's fast-paced world, where stress seems to be an inevitable part of daily life, finding effective ways to manage stress is crucial. One often overlooked yet vital component of stress management is nutrition. The food we eat affects our emotional and physical well-being. You can manage your stress levels and improve your overall health by changing what you eat and following some simple nutritional guidelines.

MAINTAINING A BALANCED DIET

A balanced diet with nutritious meals supports your emotional and physical health. Eating various whole foods, including fruits, vegetables, whole grains, and lean proteins, gives your body the essential nutrients it needs to fight against stress. Fruits and vegetables are particularly rich in vitamins, minerals, and antioxidants, which combat oxidative stress—a byproduct of chronic stress (Rahaman et al., 2023). For instance, vitamin C found in citrus fruits lowers cortisol levels, the hormone associated with stress, reducing its impact on the body (Travers, 2022).

Eating whole grains like brown rice, oats, and quinoa is a great way to keep your energy levels steady throughout the day. These grains provide complex carbohydrates that prevent sudden spikes and drops in blood sugar, which can make you feel more stressed and tired (The Ultimate Guide to Whole Grains, 2021). Whole grains support stable energy levels throughout the day, essential for maintaining a calm and focused mind. Lean proteins, including chicken, fish, beans, and legumes, are necessary to produce neurotransmitters like serotonin, which helps regulate mood and promote well-being.

CREATING A HEALTHY EATING PLAN

Planning and preparing healthy meals ensures that your body receives the proper nutrition and promotes long-term health and stress management. Meal planning involves selecting different nutrient-dense foods and organizing weekly meals in advance. This minimizes the temptation to reach for convenient but unhealthy options during busy or stressful times. Preparing meals in advance, such as cooking large batches of soups, stews, or casseroles, can save you time and reduce the likelihood of skipping meals or making poor dietary choices.

Planning and preparing your meals ahead of time can help you establish a routine that supports your nutritional needs. To ensure your body gets all the nutrients it needs, include a mix of colorful vegetables, whole grains, and lean proteins in your meals. Additionally, readily available healthy snacks like nuts, seeds, and fresh fruit can help you maintain steady energy levels and prevent the urge to indulge in stress-inducing foods.

NUTRIENT-RICH FOODS

Eating foods rich in vitamins, minerals, and antioxidants can enhance your mood and increase your energy levels, making it easier to cope with stress. Antioxidant-rich foods, such as berries, dark leafy greens, and nuts, protect the body from oxidative damage caused by free radicals (Natural Sources of Antioxidants, 2019). These foods improve your physical health and promote mental clarity and emotional stability. Blueberries, for example, are high in antioxidants known as flavonoids, which can improve cognitive function and reduce symptoms of anxiety and depression (Benefits of Blueberries on the Brain Health, 2024).

Omega-3 fatty acids, found in fatty fish like salmon, walnuts, and flaxseeds, have anti-inflammatory properties and support brain health (Hjalmarsdottir, 2018). These healthy fats play a crucial role in maintaining cell membrane integrity and facilitating communication between brain cells. Eating foods rich in omega-3 can lower anxiety levels and improve mood regulation.

B vitamins, such as B6, B12, and folate, are vital in energy production and neurotransmitter synthesis. Eating foods rich in these vitamins, like eggs, poultry, leafy greens, and legumes, supports the body's energy levels and promotes healthy brain function, which can alleviate stress. Studies show that a deficiency in B vitamins leads to heightened stress and a high risk of depression (Jahan-Mihan et al., 2024).

THE EFFECTS OF EATING STRESS-INDUCING FOODS

Managing stress also involves steering clear of stress-inducing foods and drinks. Certain foods and drinks can exacerbate anxiety and negatively impact your overall well-being. High-caffeine beverages, such as coffee and energy drinks, can increase heart rate and blood pressure, leading to heightened feelings of uncertainty and restlessness. While moderate caffeine intake can be part of a healthy diet, try minimizing your caffeine intake, especially during stressful periods.

Refined sugars and processed foods, often found in sweets, pastries, and fast food, can cause sharp fluctuations in blood sugar levels, leading to irritability, mood swings, and heightened stress (Petre, 2019). Choosing natural sweeteners like fruit and focusing on whole, unprocessed foods can help stabilize blood sugar and support a more balanced mood.

Many people use alcohol as a coping mechanism when they feel stressed; however, alcohol can have a depressant effect on the central nervous system and interfere with sleep quality (Why You Shouldn't Rely on Alcohol during Times of Stress, 2020). This disruption can add to stress and anxiety. Instead of reaching for a drink, try drinking water or herbal teas to help your body cope with stress better.

SLEEP HYGIENE

Good sleep hygiene is another effective stress-management technique. One of the most important practices is establishing a consistent sleep schedule, which helps regulate the body's internal clock. Our bodies thrive on routine, and sticking to regular sleep and wake times can significantly improve how you cope with stress.

Here are a few strategies to improve your sleep hygiene:

- **Create a consistent sleep schedule:** This involves going to bed and waking up at the same time every day, including weekends. Regularity aligns the body's circadian rhythm—the natural sleep and wake cycle. When your internal clock

is in sync, you experience more restful and restorative sleep, which enables you to handle stress and daily challenges better.
- **Develop a calming bedtime routine:** Many people struggle with insomnia or frequent night awakenings. Engaging in relaxing activities before bed, such as reading, a warm bath, or practicing gentle yoga, signals the body that it's time to unwind. A consistent pre-sleep routine helps you fall asleep faster and ensures deeper, more refreshing sleep.
- **Reduce screen time before bed:** Electronic devices like smartphones and tablets emit blue light, suppressing melatonin—the hormone that regulates sleep. Experts recommend avoiding screens for at least an hour before bedtime to allow natural melatonin production and promote easier sleep onset (Cooper, 2022). This practice also helps reduce mental stimulation, making it easier to relax.

Incorporating relaxation techniques into your nightly routine can also enhance your sleep. Practices like diaphragmatic breathing, progressive muscle relaxation, or guided imagery help calm the mind and body, making it easier to drift into sleep. For instance, deep breathing slows the heart rate and creates a sense of calm, preparing you for a peaceful night's rest.

THE BENEFITS OF SLEEP HYGIENE

Prioritizing sleep hygiene profoundly affects stress management and emotional regulation, enhancing your overall health.

Sleep is essential to lead a healthier, more balanced life. Here are a few benefits of getting adequate sleep:

- **Better heart health:** Sleep is vital for maintaining heart health by regulating blood pressure and reducing inflammation.

- **Weight management:** Quality sleep helps regulate hormones related to appetite, making it easier to manage a healthy weight.
- **Stronger immune system:** Adequate sleep boosts the immune system, making the body more resistant to infections.
- **Improved athletic performance:** Restful sleep enhances physical abilities, reaction time, and overall fitness.
- **Improves brain function:** Getting adequate sleep helps your brain process emotions, reducing anxiety and irritability during stressful times.

KEY TAKEAWAYS

Unhealthy habits and emotional responses often trigger stress. Learning to manage it effectively is crucial in breaking negative patterns and developing positive habits.

Living an active lifestyle enhances your physical health and helps you manage stress better. Simple activities like running, swimming, or even taking short walks throughout the day can go a long way in relieving stress. Find activities you enjoy and make them a part of your daily routine, and watch your emotional regulation and overall well-being improve.

Proper nutrition also helps regulate mood, increases energy levels, and improves brain function, all of which directly influence how you respond to stress. Making healthier food choices like eating whole, unprocessed foods and incorporating nutrients like B vitamins, healthy fats, and antioxidants nourishes your body and mind. Avoiding refined sugars and processed foods can stabilize blood sugar, prevent irritability, and promote a sense of balance, making it easier to manage daily challenges without reverting to toxic behaviors.

Equally important is the role of sleep hygiene. Establishing a consistent sleep routine and creating a calming pre-sleep ritual allows the body to rest and recover fully. Good sleep improves emotional regulation, reduces anxiety, and enhances your resilience to stress. By prioritizing sleep, you equip yourself with the mental clarity and energy needed to replace harmful habits with healthier coping mechanisms.

Exercise, nutrition, and sleep hygiene form a strong foundation for stress management. They provide you with the physical and emotional resources to handle the complexities of change, helping you build a more positive and balanced life. While change can be challenging, these essential practices empower you to approach each step with greater resilience, patience, and self-compassion.

CHAPTER 11
COMMUNICATION SKILLS IN TEXTING

Words are, of course, the most powerful drug used by mankind.

RUDYARD KIPLING

Ah, texting—modern-day communication's double-edged sword. On the one hand, it allows us to stay connected instantly; on the other, it can be a breeding ground for misunderstandings, passive aggression, and some seriously toxic behaviors. If you've ever fired off an angry text only to regret it 0.2 seconds later, welcome to the club. We've all been there.

Let me paint a picture: Once, during a heated argument via text, I thought I'd "win" by sending a barrage of dramatic one-liners, each in its separate message (because that gets the point across, right?). It started with "I just can't do this anymore..." followed by "You never listen to me," and the pièce de résistance: "Fine. Whatever."

After a few minutes of radio silence, I felt victorious. That is until I got hit with a single, soul-crushing response: "K"

That's when I knew this was not my finest moment. Toxic texting had claimed yet another victim: my dignity.

The truth is that communication through text can be a minefield, especially when emotions are running high. The good news is that there are strategies you can use to avoid the traps of toxic communication habits and develop healthier, more effective ways to communicate. Trust me, no one wins in a passive-aggressive text battle, not even the person who sends the last message.

DEVELOPING EFFECTIVE COMMUNICATION SKILLS

Whether talking to someone in person or texting them, improving your communication skills requires mindfulness and planning. In today's fast-paced world, texting is one of the most common forms of interaction, yet it often leads to misunderstandings due to the lack of emotional context. Practicing mindfulness can transform how you text, making your conversations clearer, more positive, and more productive.

Below are some techniques that can help you approach conversation respectfully and empathetically:

PAUSE AND REFLECT

Taking a moment before responding can significantly improve your communication skills, especially in texting. While texting is a convenient and widely used way to connect, it's also notorious for leading to misunderstandings and conflicts. One minute, you think you're being witty, and the next, you're in a full-blown argument over an emoji that was "misinterpreted."

Simply pausing and reflecting before hitting send can reduce the chances of miscommunication and maintain healthier conversations.

Text messages are tricky because they lack the emotional cues we rely on in face-to-face interactions. There's no body language, facial expressions, or tone of voice to help clarify meaning. I remember sending a joke to a friend once, fully expecting them to laugh. Instead, all I got was a flat "Okay." Ouch. Lesson learned: sarcasm doesn't always translate through text. Pausing before replying can help you step back and think, "Will they get the joke, or do I need to clarify?" Studies show that taking a brief pause before replying can minimize confusion and lead to clearer communication, especially when emotions are running high (Dearnell, 2022).

Pausing before responding gives you time to cool down, manage those immediate emotions, and consider how your words might be received. Sometimes, texting makes us emotional, especially in heated arguments or sensitive topics. Taking a pause allows you to control your emotions and come to the conversation with a clear head. This calm moment helps you rewrite or clarify your message, ensuring your intentions are understood.

Here are some proven strategies to help you improve your text communication:

BE MINDFUL OF WHO YOU ARE TEXTING

Always be mindful of who you're texting and who might see the message. For example, avoid using slang, abbreviations, or emojis when texting your boss. And if you have a problem with someone, it's better to talk to them directly or send a private message instead of discussing it in a group chat.

Also, consider the recipient's perspective before hitting send. Understanding their context, mood, and potential reactions is crucial for effective communication. You can craft a more empathetic and thoughtful message by putting yourself in their shoes. This approach helps bridge gaps in understanding and promotes meaningful connections, ensuring that your communication isn't just about speaking but genuinely connecting with others.

CHOOSE THE RIGHT MEDIUM

Before you hit send on that message, consider if texting is the best way to get your point across. Texting is casual and can lack the personal touch, so it might not be the best choice to ask someone to marry you or resign from your job. If you find yourself spending a lot of time crafting your message, it might be worth considering sending an email, giving them a call, or meeting up face-to-face instead.

AVOID USING ALL CAPS

It's generally best to avoid typing in all capital letters when sending texts, chatting, or writing emails. Not only is it difficult to read, but it can also come across as if you are shouting or upset.

PROOFREAD BEFORE SENDING

Before you hit send on any text message, double-check for any spelling mistakes, grammar errors, or auto-correct mishaps. These little slip-ups can confuse the person you're messaging. It's also important to ensure you're sending the message to the right person. Once you've hit that send button, there's no going back!

DON'T JUMP TO CONCLUSIONS

Texting can be tricky because messages don't always convey tone or context. For instance, if someone responds to your message with just a single letter like "k," don't automatically think they're being rude or uninterested. They may just be busy, or their phone battery might be running low. If you're unsure about the meaning behind a message, it's always better to ask for clarification or even give them a call to avoid misunderstandings.

RESPECT TEXTING ETIQUETTE

Being respectful in your messages prevents misunderstandings and ensures your point comes across clearly. When texting, consider the following guidelines:

- **Avoid texting at odd hours:** Be mindful of time when texting someone. Sending a message in the middle of the night and expecting an immediate response can be disruptive and inconsiderate. People have different sleep schedules, and while your message might not seem urgent, it could disturb someone's rest. It's even more crucial for work-related messages to respect boundaries by sticking to business hours unless it's urgent. If it's something that can wait until the morning, it's always better to delay sending the message. You can also use scheduling features to send it at an appropriate time.

- **Stay respectful:** Text communication, like all forms of interaction, requires respect. Avoid gossiping, arguing, or sharing confidential information in text messages, as written words can easily be misinterpreted and shared. Digital messages can be saved, forwarded, or even screenshotted, meaning that private or sensitive information can quickly be made public. Even during disagreements, it's crucial to maintain a respectful tone and keep the conversation productive. Aggressive or disrespectful texting destroys relationships and can damage your reputation if shared with others.

- **Keep it concise:** Texts are meant to be brief and to the point. Overly long text messages can overwhelm the recipient and may cause them to miss important details. If your message requires a lengthy explanation, it might be better suited for an email, phone call, or in-person discussion. When sending a text, focus on clarity and brevity, ensuring your message is easy to read and understand. This helps the recipient respond more efficiently without feeling overwhelmed by too much information at once.

- **Reply promptly:** Timely responses help maintain clear communication. If you receive a text and can't provide a full reply immediately, send a quick note explaining the delay. For instance, if you're in a meeting or handling something urgent, a message like, "I'm tied up right now, but I'll get back to you as soon as I'm free," is courteous and lets the sender know you've received their message. Prompt responses show respect for the other person's time and demonstrate your reliability in communication.

- **Focus on real-life conversations:** Texting while talking to someone face-to-face can seem disrespectful and give the impression that you're not interested in the current conversation. If you absolutely must attend to a message, explain why you need to divert your attention. For example, you might say, "I'm expecting an important update about my family member's health, so I need to check my phone." This lets the other person know it's a unique circumstance, not just a lack of respect for their time.
- **Be culturally sensitive:** Different cultures have varying norms when it comes to communication styles, including texting. In some cultures, messages may be more formal, while others might be more casual. Understanding these nuances prevents misunderstandings and ensures your texts are received as intended. For instance, using emojis or slang may be acceptable with friends but could be seen as unprofessional or disrespectful in a more formal or multicultural setting. Be aware of how different groups communicate and adjust your style accordingly.
- **Refrain from texting someone with sad news or breaking up with them:** Having these conversations in person or over the phone is more personal and respectful. It shows that you care enough to have a face-to-face discussion, allowing for better communication and understanding.

DO NOT TEXT WHILE DRIVING

Texting while driving is extremely dangerous. According to statistics, approximately 3,000 people lose their lives in car accidents in the United States every year (Bieber, 2023). In many states, texting while driving is not only dangerous but also illegal. Law enforcement agencies have enacted stricter penalties, such as heavy fines and the suspension of driver's licenses, to curb this dangerous behavior. It's better to put your phone down and focus on the road to keep everyone safe.

USE "I" STATEMENTS

Framing messages constructively is crucial for effective communication, especially when texting. How you frame your messages can greatly influence how they are received and interpreted.

Using "I" statements when texting can help you express your feelings and needs without coming across as aggressive or blaming. It reduces defensiveness, minimizes conflict, and encourages open dialogue. For example, instead of saying, "You never listen to me," which sounds accusatory and may trigger defensiveness, you could say, "I feel unheard when I talk about my day, and I need you to listen." This reframing shifts the focus from blaming the other person to sharing your perspective. It helps the recipient understand your feelings without feeling attacked, creating a more constructive and empathetic conversation. This creates a safer environment for honest expression. Being vulnerable can lead to a deeper understanding and stronger connection.

Using "I" statements also encourages a greater sense of personal responsibility in communication. Expressing how a specific situation affects you personally allows you to take ownership of your feelings and communicate them in a manner that invites empathy rather than defensiveness. For example, instead of saying, "You always cancel plans last minute," you could say, "I feel disappointed when plans change unexpectedly because I look forward to spending time with you." This approach not only communicates the emotional impact of the action but also maintains respect and invites a constructive, solution-focused conversation

APPLYING "I" STATEMENTS

Try practicing and refining this skill to make "I" statements a regular part of your texting habit. Role-playing can be a great way to get comfortable with this form of communication. You could practice with a friend or partner, simulating a situation like not receiving a reply to an important message, and respond with something like, "I felt worried when I didn't hear back from you, and I need reassurance that everything is okay." This exercise helps you articulate your feelings and needs in a clear, non-accusatory manner.

Additionally, getting feedback on your use of "I" statements can be valuable for improvement. Having honest conversations with people you trust and asking how this communication style affects them can give you insight into areas of improvement. This process of practice and feedback makes using "I" statements more natural and effective in your everyday interactions over time.

CHECK IN WITH YOURSELF

Evaluating your emotional state before texting is critical to maintaining effective communication and avoiding unnecessary conflict. Taking a moment to assess how you feel before responding can help you avoid sending emotionally charged messages that may escalate a situation rather than resolve it.

Before you press send:

- **Check in with yourself:** Are you feeling angry, frustrated, or upset? Recognizing these emotions and their potential impact on your message is crucial. When emotions are high, there's a greater chance of saying something you'll regret. This self-awareness allows you to pause and reconsider whether your current emotional state might lead to a rewarding or harmful exchange.
- **Avoid impulsive, emotion-driven messages:** Stepping back before you respond helps you approach conversations with clarity and intention, resulting in more respectful and meaningful interactions. This practice improves immediate conversation and builds healthier long-term communication habits.
- **Practice mindfulness before texting:** Taking a few deep breaths and calming your mind before engaging in a conversation allows you to reduce the intensity of your emotions and gain a more balanced perspective. Research

suggests that mindfulness improves emotional regulation by increasing emotional awareness and acceptance (Schuman-Olivier et al., 2020).
- **Incorporate self-assessment tools or prompts:** Asking yourself simple questions like "How am I feeling right now?" or "Is this the best time to respond?" can create a necessary pause, helping you craft a more thoughtful and appropriate reply. Reflecting on these prompts gives you the space to ensure your response aligns with your intentions and avoids unnecessary conflict.
- **Wait until you're calm before responding:** If your initial reaction is driven by strong negative emotions, give yourself time to cool down. Wait a few minutes, hours, or even until the next day. The goal isn't to ignore or suppress your feelings but to allow them to settle, ensuring you can constructively express yourself without damaging the relationship. Mindfully handling emotions will enable you to communicate in ways that build understanding rather than conflict.

Regularly reflecting on your emotions can help you build emotional awareness. This can go beyond just texting and become a natural habit. Checking in with your feelings allows you to recognize and understand your emotional triggers. This self-awareness enhances your communication skills, making you more understanding and considerate in your interactions.

Mindfulness-based techniques are particularly effective in this regard. Mindfulness promotes greater awareness and acceptance of your emotional states and enhances emotional regulation. This leads to improved decision-making and reduced likelihood of reacting impulsively under stress. Practicing mindfulness regularly equips you with the tools you need to manage your emotions better, not just in texting but in all forms of communication.

Incorporating mindfulness into your everyday life doesn't have to be complicated. Just try simple things like taking deep breaths, doing body scans, or taking a few minutes to meditate. Consistency will bring out the best in you over time. By making these practices a regular part of your routine, you'll start to notice a positive change. As you continue, you'll become more aware of your emotions and better equipped to deal with them healthily.

KEY TAKEAWAYS

Effective communication skills play a crucial role in all aspects of communication. Texting is integral to modern communication, but its limitations, such as the absence of non-verbal cues, can lead to misunderstandings and conflicts. By incorporating mindfulness into your texting habits, you can significantly enhance the clarity and intent behind your messages.

Taking a moment to pause before responding to a text allows you to assess your emotional state, ensuring that you are not reacting impulsively to triggers that may arise. You can approach conversations with a balanced perspective by grounding yourself in the present moment, leading to more thoughtful and respectful exchanges. This mindfulness practice is crucial, especially in emotionally charged discussions, as it helps to de-escalate tensions and encourages a healthier communication environment.

Additionally, using "I" statements allows you to express your feelings and needs without assigning blame. This approach reduces defensiveness and encourages open dialogue, paving the way for deeper understanding and connection. When you take responsibility for your emotions and frame your messages constructively, you invite empathy from others and create a space for meaningful conversations.

As you practice the strategies we discussed in this chapter, remember that communication is a skill that can be honed over time. Mindfulness is a powerful tool that empowers you to communicate with intention and awareness, significantly enhancing the quality of your interactions. Practicing these techniques consistently cultivates healthier relationships and can dramatically improve your emotional well-being.

Effective communication through texting is not just about

exchanging information; it's about connecting with others on a deeper level. Embracing mindfulness in your texting habits allows you to handle the complexities of modern communication with grace and compassion. As you move forward, carry these insights with you and let them guide your conversations, ensuring that every message you send is thoughtful, transparent, and reflects your true intentions.

FREE BONUS

You've made it close to the end and you deserve a round of applause. Your journey through the "How to Stop Being Toxic Playbook" started with you. You were brave, open-minded and willing. Amazing work!

By now, you're probably noticed your toxic behaviors and learned how to tackle them. Pat yourself on the back because I'm so proud. All I can hope for is to wish you the best in the future - a positive shift in your mindset and walking away from toxic patterns that don't serve you.

To keep you on track and motivated for the final stretch, I've put together a bonus package just for you: a toxic behavior elimination checklist, a relationship reset guide and so much more.

Trust me, these tools are worthy and meant to equip you with the knowledge to keep you pushing forward as a change person.

To access your free bonus, type **(https://emotionalhealthbooks.com/howtostopbeingtoxic-free-bonus)** into your browser, or just scan the QR code below and tap the link—it's that simple.

Thank you for staying focused and remember, you got this. I'm so proud of the progress you've made.

Keep it up, and let's finish this transformation strong!

BEFORE WE WRAP UP YOUR TRANSFORMATION

I have a quick favor to ask: Would you be willing to leave an honest review on this book?

Whether good or bad, I appreciate all comments given.

Your feedback will go a long way in helping others who are ready to break free from toxic behaviors and build healthier connections.

Inspiring someone to start their own journey toward personal growth and emotional health is the first step. That step and credit goes to you so let me be the one to say thank you. All it took was one kind but honest review.

To make it easy, just scan the QR code below, and it'll take you straight to the review page. Or, if you prefer, head to your Amazon orders page, find the book, and click "Write a review" below the product details.

>> **Leave a review on Amazon US** <<

>> Leave a review on Amazon UK <<

Thank you so much for your time and support! You are the reason I write.

Wayne Waters

CONCLUSION

Growth is an erratic forward movement: two steps forward, one step back. Remember that and be very gentle with yourself.

JULIA CAMERON

As we wrap up this journey, picture this: It's your best friend's birthday party, and the cake is an absolute masterpiece. You're eyeing that last slice, envisioning the perfect blend of frosting and cake, when suddenly, a friend swoops in, forks raised, claiming it as their own.

At that moment, you face a choice: Do you unleash your inner cake monster, throw a tantrum worthy of a toddler, or take a deep breath and approach the situation gracefully? Perhaps you summon the courage to say, "I feel really disappointed when the last slice disappears before I get a chance to enjoy it. Can we find a way to share it next time?"

This scenario illustrates a common struggle most of us face—managing our reactions and expressing our feelings without resorting to toxic behaviors. Like that last slice of cake, our emotions can be sweet, but if not handled properly, they can turn sour. As we conclude this book, let's take that lesson to heart: navigating life's challenges, whether they're about cake or more profound issues, requires patience, self-awareness, and a bit of humor.

As you move forward, reflect on the 60 practical techniques explored throughout this book and how you can implement them in your life. From self-awareness to mastering communication and managing stress, every chapter has equipped you with actionable tools to guide you toward positive transformation.

Now, let's dive into our final thoughts on embracing personal growth and cultivating healthier relationships:

The first key takeaway is understanding the root of toxic behavior. Toxicity often stems from unresolved trauma, emotional pain, or deep-seated thinking and behavior patterns. Recognizing this is crucial. Awareness is the first step toward change, and by reflecting on your actions and acknowledging toxic tendencies, you can start working on changing those habits. Importantly, this journey requires self-compassion, accepting your flaws without judgment, and knowing that recognizing them is a strength, not a weakness.

Effective communication is another pillar of this transformation. Poor communication causes many conflicts and misunderstandings in relationships. Learning to express yourself clearly and practicing active listening can significantly improve your interactions. Remember, communication is as much about understanding as it is about being understood.

Managing stress is also essential for curbing toxic behaviors. Stress often amplifies negative reactions, making minor problems feel overwhelming. By integrating stress-management techniques like mindfulness, exercise, and time management into your life, you can maintain a calmer, more balanced mindset, allowing you to respond to challenges with clarity and thoughtfulness.

Building meaningful connections takes intention and effort. Relationships thrive when nurtured with kindness, empathy, and mutual respect. Make a conscious decision to be fully present, express appreciation, and be supportive in your relationships. Small acts of kindness can strengthen your connections and create a more positive environment for your relationships to flourish.

Self-care is another cornerstone of personal growth. Taking care of your physical, emotional, and mental well-being sets the stage for a healthier, more fulfilling life. Prioritize activities that bring joy, practice self-compassion, and establish healthy boundaries. Remember, self-care isn't selfish; you must be your best self for those around you.

Now that you've explored these techniques, it's time to implement them. Maybe you're wondering, *Where do I begin?* Start with one or two strategies that resonate most and gradually incorporate more. Change takes time; be patient with yourself. Celebrate the small wins along the way and stay focused on your goals.

Commit yourself to change. Dedicate the next year to embracing and applying the strategies outlined in this playbook. Give yourself the time and space for transformation. This playbook can be a guide that you revisit throughout your journey, revealing new insights each time.

Changing your behavior and improving your relationships is an ongoing journey. Challenges will arise, but remember that every step, no matter how small, is progress. Setbacks are natural; use them as opportunities to learn, adapt, and keep moving forward.

Acknowledge the hard work you've put in and reward yourself for your dedication. Staying motivated doesn't have to be all business, no play. Make time to celebrate your achievements. Let it inspire you to keep going, no matter how small the victory is.

Most importantly, believe in your ability to change. You have the power within you to transform your life and create healthier, more meaningful relationships. Trust the process and your capacity for growth. By engaging with this playbook, you've already shown your willingness to make positive changes, and that alone is a huge step forward.

Finally, I want to commend you for your courage and willingness to transform your life. Remember that personal growth is a lifelong journey. There's always room for improvement, learning, and adaptation. Embrace change with a positive mindset, and you'll handle life's challenges gracefully.

Let me leave you with this thought: Focus on the process, not the prize. The ultimate goal is impressive, but the journey will appear like a movie. The effort you put into and the lessons learned along the way only lead to better outcomes, so take time to appreciate each step. You have started on a transformative journey. With faith in yourself, anything is possible.

You've got this!

REFERENCES

Bach, R. (n.d.). *The bond that links your true family is not one of blood but of respect and joy in each other's life.* https://psychicblaze.com/family-inspirational-quotes/#google_vignette

Brown, B. (2021, April 5). *58 positive discipline quotes to help you show your love.* Abundance Mindset Mama. https://abundancemindsetmama.com/positive-discipline-quotes

Deneault, A.-A., Nivison, M., & Madigan, S. (2023, October 19). *How children's secure attachment sets the stage for positive well-being.* The Conversation. https://theconversation.com/how-childrens-secure-attachment-sets-the-stage-for-positive-well-being

Elbeltagi, R., Al-Beltagi, M., Saeed, N. K., & Alhawamdeh, R. (2023). Play therapy in children with autism: Its role, implications, and limitations. *World Journal of Clinical Pediatrics, 12*(1), 1–22. https://www.ncbi.nlm.nih.gov/pmc/articles/PMC9850869/

Engel, B. (2016). *The power of apology.* Psychology Today. https://www.psychologytoday.com/us/articles/200207/the-power-apology

Ford, T. (n.d.). *The most important things in life are the connections you make with others.* https://www.happierhuman.com/connection-quotes/

Gowmon, V. (2019, May 29). *Inspiring Quotes on Child Learning and Development.* Vince Gowmon. https://www.vincegowmon.com/inspiring-quotes-on-child-learning-and-development/

Guy-Evans, O. (2022, November 3). *What is dopamine in the brain.* Simply Psychology. https://www.simplypsychology.org/the-role-of-dopamine-as-a-neurotransmitter-in-the-human-brain.html#

InBrief: The science of early childhood development. (n.d.). Center on the Developing Child at Harvard University. https://developingchild.harvard.edu/resources/inbrief-science-of-ecd/

Karni-Visel, Y., Hershkowitz, I., Lamb, M. E., & Blasbalg, U. (2021). Nonverbal emotions while disclosing child abuse: The role of interviewer support. *Child Maltreatment, 28*(1), 107755952110634. https://doi.org/10.1177/10775595211063497

Kim, A., Panisara Sutthipong, Mya LeVaughn, & Nicole Danielle Osier. (2023). Brain chemicals that make us happy or sad. *Frontiers for Young Minds, 11.* https://doi.org/10.3389/frym.2023.1023491

King Jr., M. L. (n.d.). *Forgiveness is not an occasional act, it is a constant attitude.* Goalcast. https://www.goalcast.com/forgiveness-quotes/

McCullough, M. E. (2024). *Forgiveness: Who does it and how do they do it? Journal Article.* Apa.org. https://psycnet.apa.org/record/2001-05842-002

Miller, B. (2024, September 9). *50 parenting quotes to inspire and guide.* Mental Health Center Kids; Mental Health Center Kids. https://mentalhealthcenterkids.com/blogs/articles/parenting-quotes#

Morin, A. (2024). *How positive reinforcement encourages good behavior in kids.* Parents. https://www.parents.com/positive-reinforcement-examples-8619283

Raj, P., Elizabeth, C. S., & Padmakumari, P. (2016). Mental health through forgiveness:

Exploring the roots and benefits. *Cogent Psychology, 3*(1). https://doi.org/10.1080/23311908.2016.1153817

Richard. (2023, April 20). *The value of teaching your child to be financially responsible.* Sprott Learning Kids -. https://sprottlearning.com/kids/the-value-of-teaching-your-child-to-be-financially-responsible/

Science-backed benefits of practicing gratitude with kids. (2019). Housmaninstitute.com. https://www.housmaninstitute.com/blog/science-backed-benefits-of-practicing-gratitude-with-kids

Shabbir, R. (2024, February 22). *20 math games that make math learning fun.* Educationise. https://educationise.com/post/20-math-games-that-make-math-learning-fun/

Tauscher, S. (2019, May 29). *Inspiring quotes on child learning and development.* Vince Gowmon. https://www.vincegowmon.com/inspiring-quotes-on-child-learning-and-development/

Van der Wal, R. C., Levelt, L., Kluwer, E., & Finkenauer, C. (2024). Exploring associations between children's forgiveness following parental divorce and psychological well-being. *Family Transitions,* 1–23. https://doi.org/10.1080/28375300.2024.2310432

Williamson. (2023, August 21). *Unlocking the power of play-based learning: 20 engaging activities for holistic development.* School Life Diaries. https://schoollifediaries.com/play-based-learning/

Made in the USA
Monee, IL
08 June 2025